Celebrate with Kim-Joy

CUTE CAKES AND BAKES TO MAKE EVERY OCCASION JOYFUL

Celebrate with Kim-Joy

CUTE CAKES AND BAKES TO MAKE EVERY OCCASION JOYFUL

PHOTOGRAPHY BY ELLIS PARRINDER
ILLUSTRATIONS BY LINDA VAN DEN BERG
LETTERING DESIGN BY MARY KATE MᶜDEVITT

Hardie Grant

QUADRILLE

Contents

Introduction

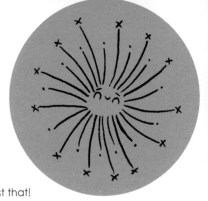

When I think of celebrations, I think of food, colour and joy. So this book is full of just that! Unique, delicious and joyful recipes for different occasions, including all the universal celebrations like birthdays and weddings, but also important celebrations from around the world, like Lunar New Year, Day of the Dead and Holi.

One of my favourite things about baking is how it brings people together, so that's why I've included some recipes that are a departure from the norm to encourage creativity and conversation. For instance, birthday bakes don't have to be just cake! So while I have included traditional tiered cakes, I've also included bakes like Kagekone, a Danish pastry where the head is pulled off and traditionally everyone screams! (page 44); and a dinosaur-themed burnt Basque cheesecake which is extremely easy to make but oh so delicious (page 42). There are unique and varied recipes throughout, from wedding breads like Korovai (page 108) and a festive Kransekake (page 94) to Valentine's robot fondant fancies (page 57).

There's also a mix of difficulty levels across all the bakes, and while of course everything is decorated fit for a celebration, it is easy to simplify or leave out the decorations on all the recipes. There are also step-by-step images to guide you through key stages, and vegan and gluten-free versions throughout so that your celebrations can cater for everyone!

Each recipe is designed for a specific celebration, but many of these could be used for different celebrations with easy tweaks. For instance, the Christmas Cookies (page 84) could be decorated differently for a birthday or snack at a wedding; the Edible Cat Terrarium (page 39) could be made into a Christmas, Halloween or even Bonfire Night version (imagine a little bonfire scene inside the terrarium!). The Valentine's Robot Fondant Fancies (page 57) could be Festive Robot Fancies for Christmas, or menacing Halloween versions. The Space Turtle Croquembouche (page 101) would happily be eaten at any celebration. You can vary the flavours to suit the celebration! There are endless possibilities.

Most importantly, I want you to enjoy the process of baking and creating – so try the recipes that bring you the most happiness, and feel free to alter them to suit you. We often think of baking as a science, and while there is a science to baking, there is also flexibility and fun. Things may not go quite to plan, but you adapt as you go along to make things work for you. You never know, you might create something original and wonderful! New ideas often come out of mistakes, not through achieving perfection! Maybe your cake is wonky – so why not carve into it and turn it into a feature? Maybe you burn your cake (oh no!) – but cut the burnt bits off, soak the remaining cake with simple syrup, decorate it and no one will be any the wiser. Maybe your edible house doesn't quite fit together – but you use extra store-bought or homemade cookies to pad it out and make it work! Baking can go wrong, even when you're experienced, but as long as you enjoy the process and stay flexible, it will bring a smile to you and the lucky recipients!

CELEBRATE AND SPREAD JOY THROUGH YOUR BAKING!

Kim-Joy

Basics

Vanilla Cake

This is my go-to plain vanilla cake recipe, which you can then flavour however you like! Here are just some of the flavours you can play about with in this recipe: citrus zest (for this quantity I'd use the zest of 3–4 fruits), almond extract, freeze-dried fruit powders, orange blossom water, rose water, liqueurs, lavender and spices, such as cinnamon, cardamon, etc. You can also layer this cake up with your choice of fresh fruits, homemade curd, crème pâtissière, caramel, etc!

SERVES: 25–30 (MAKES: 5 X 18-CM [7-IN] CAKES)

480g [2 cups plus 2 Tbsp] unsalted butter, cubed, at room temperature, plus extra for greasing
480g [2½ cups minus 4 tsp] caster or granulated sugar
1 tsp salt (or use salted butter and omit this)
480g [17oz] eggs (about 8 medium)
1 Tbsp vanilla bean paste

260ml [1 cup plus 4 tsp] whole milk
200ml [¾ cup plus 2 Tbsp] whole yogurt
560g [4⅓ cups] plain [all-purpose] flour (or use gluten-free flour plus 2¼ tsp xanthan gum)
6 tsp baking powder (use gluten-free baking powder if making gluten free, a lot of standard

baking powders contain gluten)
60g [½ cup] almond flour

PLUS
fresh whipped cream and fruit

1 / Preheat the oven to 170°C [325°F/Gas mark 3]. Grease 5 x 18-cm [7-in] cake tins with butter and line the bases with baking paper.

2 / Add the butter, sugar and salt to a stand mixer (or use a handheld electric whisk) fitted with the balloon whisk attachment and whisk on medium speed until the butter is smooth, then increase the speed to high and whisk until the butter is fluffy and pale in colour.

3 / Lightly beat the eggs in a separate bowl. Add the egg mixture, 1 Tbsp at a time, to the creamed butter and sugar mixture, beating well after each addition. Add the vanilla bean paste and mix to combine.

4 / In a separate bowl, mix the milk and yogurt together. Sift the flour, baking powder and almond flour together into another bowl.

5 / Alternate between sifting in a quarter of the flours, then adding a quarter of the milk and yogurt

to the main mixture, mixing on slow speed after each addition. Be careful not to overmix and add the flour and milk when the ingredients from the batch before have only semi-mixed in. Divide the batter between the prepared cake tins and bake for 30–35 minutes until a skewer or a knife inserted in the centre comes out clean.

6 / When the cakes are baked, leave them to cool in their tins for 5 minutes, then run a knife around the edges and turn out onto wire racks. Peel off the baking paper and leave to cool.

7 / Make sure the cakes are cool before assembling – you can make 1 tall stacked cake or 2 shorter cakes. Decorate simply with fresh cream and fruit between the layers OR follow one of the basic cake designs on pages 15, 18 and 21, or the elaborate designs on pages 36, 67, 105, 127, 138, 159 and 163.

Ginger Cake

This ginger cake never fails to impress – soft, fluffy and moist, this is a loud and proud ginger cake made with ground ginger plus additional crystallized stem ginger for extra bursts of flavour. This quantity makes a 5-layer cake for an impressively tall celebration cake, but you can always reduce the quantity.

> This recipe makes a large quantity so you need a big bowl, although the batter can be divided in half if you like.

SERVES: 25–30 (MAKES: 5 X 18-CM [7-IN] CAKES)

CAKE
335g [1½ cups] salted butter (or use unsalted and add 1 tsp salt), plus extra for greasing
335g [1⅔ cups plus 1 tsp] dark muscovado [soft brown] sugar
160g [½ cup plus 1½ Tbsp] black treacle [molasses]
500g [3¾ cups] plain [all-purpose] flour (or use gluten-free flour plus 2 tsp xanthan gum)

3 tsp baking powder (use gluten-free baking powder if making gluten free, a lot of standard baking powders contain gluten)
5 Tbsp ground ginger
1 Tbsp ground cinnamon
400ml [1⅔ cups] whole milk
135g [¾ cup plus 1 Tbsp] crystallized stem [candied preserved] ginger, roughly chopped

5 medium eggs
2½ tsp bicarbonate of soda [baking soda]

SALTED CARAMEL
90ml [6 Tbsp] water
240g [1¼ cups plus 2 tsp] caster or granulated sugar
225ml [1 cup minus 1 Tbsp] double [heavy] cream (or coconut milk to make vegan – you won't taste the coconut flavour due

to the strong flavours of the cake)
fine table salt, to taste

PLUS
½ quantity of Dulce de Leche Buttercream (page 33)
120g [1 cup plus 1 tsp] pecans, lightly toasted and roughly chopped

1 / Preheat the oven to 160°C [325°F/Gas mark 3]. Grease 5 x 18-cm [7-in] cake tins with butter and line the bases with baking paper.

2 / For the cake, place the butter, salt (if using), sugar and treacle in a small pan and heat over a low-medium heat, stirring, until melted and combined.

3 / Combine the flour, baking powder and spices in a separate bowl.

4 / Heat the milk in a small bowl in the microwave for a minute until warm. Set aside.

5 / Pour the liquid sugar and butter mixture over the flour mixture, then stir quickly until smooth and combined. Add the chopped ginger, then the eggs, 1 at a time, mixing well after each addition.

6 / Add the bicarbonate of soda to the warm milk and mix until foamy. Pour into the main mixture and mix with a balloon whisk until just combined.

7 / Quickly pour the mix evenly among the prepared cake tins. Bake for 20–30 minutes until a knife inserted in the centre of the cake comes out clean.

8 / Meanwhile, make the salted caramel (see page 67, without the red dye). Cover with plastic wrap and freeze for 30–45 minutes. It will thicken as it cools.

9 / When the cakes are baked, leave them to cool in their tins for 5 minutes, then run a knife around the edges and turn out onto wire racks. Peel off the baking paper and leave to cool.

10 / Ensure the cakes are cool before assembling. Stack them using the guide on page 27; in between each layer, pipe an even layer of buttercream, drizzle with salted caramel and sprinkle with pecans. Pipe more buttercream on top. OR follow one of the basic cake designs on pages 15, 18 and 21, or the elaborate designs on pages 36, 67, 105, 138 and 159. If crumb-coating, ensure you use a dam (see page 27) to help contain the caramel on each layer.

Chocolate Cake

It's always great to have a go-to chocolate cake that you can use for all your cakes, so here it is – the ultimate chocolatey, moist chocolate cake. Don't skip adding the boiling water at the end – this makes the batter very liquidy (that's normal!) and helps dissolve the cocoa powder and incorporate it into the batter. The extra moisture also helps to produce a soft and unbelievably moist cake. The coffee adds depth of flavour to the chocolate, but the actual coffee flavour will be undetectable, so don't worry if you're not a coffee fan! This cake is very soft and moist. It will still stack, but just be careful if using it for the wedding cake on page 105 – it's better to use it on the top tier rather than on the lower ones.

> This recipe makes a large quantity so you need a big bowl, although the batter can be divided in half if you like.

SERVES: 20–25 (MAKES: 4 X 18-CM [7-IN] CAKES)

250ml [1 cup plus 2 tsp] vegetable oil, plus extra for oiling

300ml [1¼ cups] whole milk, at room temperature or warmed in the microwave for 1 minute

1½ Tbsp lemon juice

650g [3¼ cups] caster or granulated sugar

440g [3⅓ cups plus 1 tsp] plain [all-purpose] flour (or use gluten-free flour plus 2 tsp xanthan gum)

2 tsp baking powder (use gluten-free baking powder if making gluten free – a lot of standard baking powders contain gluten)

2 tsp bicarbonate of soda [baking soda]

1 tsp salt

135g [1⅓ cups] unsweetened cocoa powder, sifted (for the best results, use a high-quality Dutch-processed cocoa powder)

130ml [½ cup plus 2 tsp] sour cream (or whole yogurt)

1 Tbsp vanilla bean paste

5 medium eggs

1 Tbsp instant coffee granules (you can't taste the coffee, but leave it out if you're coffee averse)

440ml [2 cups minus 2 Tbsp] boiling water

Optional: For those of you who love chocolate and want an extra depth of flavour, you can add 70g [½ cup] cacao nibs to the batter before baking. These don't add any extra sweetness, but add intense bursts of pure chocolate flavour.

1 / 1 Preheat the oven to 160°C [325°F/Gas mark 3]. Oil 4 x 18-cm [7-in] cake tins and line the bases with a circle of baking paper.

2 / Put the milk into a large bowl and squeeze in the lemon juice. Set aside for now.

3 / Mix the sugar, flour, baking powder, bicarbonate of soda, salt and cocoa powder in a separate bowl.

4 / Add the sour cream, vegetable oil, vanilla and eggs to the milk mixture. Whisk to break up the eggs. The oil will separate, but that's fine.

5 / Put the coffee granules into a heatproof bowl and pour in the boiling water. Stir and set aside.

6 / Pour the egg mixture onto the dry ingredients and whisk until partially mixed. Add the hot coffee and whisk again until everything is combined. Divide the batter between the prepared tins and bake for 40 minutes, or until the cakes slightly come away from the sides of the tins and a skewer inserted into the centre of a cake comes out with just a few crumbs clinging to it. Leave to cool in the tins for 10 minutes before turning out onto a wire rack, peeling off the baking paper and leaving to cool completely.

7 / Make sure the cakes are cool before assembling. Stack and crumb-coat them (see pages 27–28) using your buttercream. You can can make 1 tall stacked cake or 2 shorter cakes OR follow one of the cake designs on pages 15, 18 and 21, or the elaborate designs on pages 36, 67, 105, 124, 138, 159 and 184.

Crème Brûlée Cake

This cake is made using the reverse creaming method, rather than creaming the butter and sugar together at the start, which gives it a very tender and moist crumb. The cake itself is also very white in colour because it uses oil in addition to butter, and just egg whites. Don't worry about your egg yolks going to waste: they will be used in the crème pâtissière filling! All the cakes in this book benefit from using cake flour instead of plain [all purpose] flour (see page 29), but this cake, in particular, really benefits from it if you can get your hands on a pack!

SERVES: 25–30 (MAKES: 5 X 18-CM [7-IN] CAKES)

CRÈME PÂTISSIÈRE FILLING
480ml [2 cups] whole milk
90g [½ cup minus 2 tsp] caster or granulated sugar
25g [¼ cup] cornflour [cornstarch]
1 Tbsp vanilla bean paste
7 medium egg yolks
50g [3½ Tbsp] salted butter (or use unsalted plus a pinch of salt), at room temperature, cubed

EGG WHITE MIXTURE
8 medium egg whites
200g [1 cup] caster or granulated sugar

CAKE
310g [1⅓ cups plus 2 tsp] salted butter (or use unsalted plus 1 tsp salt), at room temperature and soft, plus extra for greasing
690g [5⅓ cups] plain [all-purpose] flour
490g [2½ cups minus 2 tsp] caster or granulated sugar
2⅓ Tbsp baking powder
490ml [2 cups plus 1 Tbsp] whole milk
200ml [¾ cup plus 2 Tbsp] vegetable oil
2 Tbsp vanilla bean paste
2½ Tbsp white wine vinegar

PLUS
grated nutmeg (in between cake layers)

edible gold paint (optional)
edible gold leaf (optional)
3 Tbsp caster or granulated sugar, for the top

Tip: The butter for the cake must be at room temperature and soft and spreadable. If not, microwave it for 5 seconds at a time.

1 / First, make the crème pâtissière filling. Pour the milk into a small pan and heat over a medium heat until it comes to a simmer.

2 / While the milk is heating, place the sugar, cornflour, vanilla and egg yolks in a large heatproof bowl and whisk until thick and smooth.

3 / When the milk starts bubbling, pour it slowly into the egg mixture, whisking quickly and constantly the whole time (to temper the egg mix and ensure the eggs do not scramble!). Once all the milk is combined, pour the whole mixture back into the pan and continue heating over a medium heat. Allow the custard to bubble while whisking constantly as it thickens. If the custard starts looking lumpy at any point, just temporarily remove it from the heat and keep whisking as fast as you can.

4 / Once the custard is thick and holds a trail when the whisk is lifted from the bowl, remove from the heat and add the butter. Stir until melted and combined.

5 / Pour the custard into a bowl and cover with plastic wrap, ensuring the plastic wrap touches the surface of the custard to prevent a skin forming. Chill in the fridge for a few hours while you make the cake. It will thicken as it cools.

6 / For the cake, preheat the oven to 180°C [350°F/ Gas mark 4]. Grease 5 x 18-cm [7-in] round cake tins with butter and line the bases with a circle of baking paper.

7 / Add the egg whites to a stand mixer (or use a handheld electric whisk) fitted with a balloon whisk attachment and whisk on high speed until soft peaks form. Add the 200g [1 cup] sugar in 3 batches, whisking for 45 seconds after each addition. Transfer to another bowl and set aside for now.

8 / Place the flour in a clean stand mixer bowl, add the softened butter and, using the paddle mixer attachment, mix on slow speed for 30–60 seconds until the mixture resembles breadcrumbs. Add the 490g [2½ cups minus 2 tsp] sugar and baking powder and mix for a few seconds until just combined.

9 / Put the milk, oil, vanilla and vinegar into a microwaveable bowl and microwave on high for 1 minute 30 seconds–2 minutes until lukewarm.

10 / Add a third of the lukewarm liquid to the flour mixture and mix on slow speed until just combined. Increase the speed to high and mix for 2 minutes. Add the rest of the liquid, a third at a time, whisking on slow speed after each addition until combined.

11 / Gently fold the egg whites into the cake batter in three portions, while trying to knock out as little air as possible.

Tip: There will be extra 'crème pat' filling, but it's worth it to use up the remaining egg yolks, and you can also enjoy this on its own!

12 / Pour the batter into the prepared baking tins and bake for 40–45 minutes until a knife inserted into the centre of a cake comes out clean. Leave to cool in the tins for 5–10 minutes (the cake will shrink away from the sides a little bit, but this is normal) before running a knife around the rims and turning out onto a wire rack. Peel off the baking paper and leave to cool completely.

13 / Make sure the cakes are cool before assembling. Stack and crumb-coat the cakes (see pages 27–28) using your chosen buttercream. Use the dam technique (page 27) to add a generous amount of crème pâtissière to the centre of each layer, and grate over some nutmeg. Decorate simply with a raw edge (just don't smooth in or trim off the buttercream that collects around the sides on top). Chill the cake, then paint the raw top edge gold using edible gold paint. Add edible gold leaf to the buttercream to finish.

14 / Finish with a crème brûléed top: sprinkle the 3 Tbsp sugar over the well-chilled buttercream (pop in the freezer for 30 minutes to make sure it's chilled on top of the cake), then using a handheld blowtorch, caramelize the sugar. Be careful not to blowtorch right up to the buttercream edges, as too much will cause it to melt! OR follow one of the basic cake designs on pages 18 and 21, or the elaborate designs on 36, 67, 105, 138, 159 and 172.

Red Velvet Cake

This cake is so easy to make and rewards you with soft, fluffy and velvet-like cake. You will want more than one slice for sure.

SERVES: 20–25 (MAKES: 4 X 18-CM [7-IN] CAKE LAYERS)

This recipe makes a large quantity so you need a big bowl, although the batter can be divided in half if you like. You must bake the cake immediately after mixing the wet and dry ingredients together for the reaction (you will see the batter bubbling).

WET INGREDIENTS
butter, for greasing
450ml [2 cups minus 2 Tbsp] milk

2½ Tbsp white wine vinegar
320ml [1¼ cups plus 4 tsp] sunflower oil (or other neutral-tasting oil)
1 tsp salt
1 Tbsp vanilla bean paste
4 eggs
red gel food dye
180ml [¾ cup] boiling water

DRY INGREDIENTS
520g [4 cups] plain [all-purpose] flour

2 tsp bicarbonate of soda [baking soda]
2 tsp baking powder
700g [3½ cups] caster or granulated sugar
1½ Tbsp unsweetened cocoa powder

PLUS
1 quantity of American Buttercream (page 31) or Italian Meringue Buttercream (page 32)

1 / Preheat the oven to 170°C [340°F/Gas mark 3]. Grease the base and sides of 4 x 18-cm [7-in] cake tins with butter and line the bases with baking paper.

2 / Add the milk to a large bowl, then add the vinegar and stir (it will curdle). Set aside for now.

3 / Add all the dry ingredients to a separate large bowl, sifting in the cocoa powder, and whisk to combine.

4 / Return to the milk mixture. Add the oil, salt, vanilla bean paste and eggs and whisk to break up the eggs and combine. The oil will remain separated, but that's fine. Add red food dye to colour a deep red.

5 / Pour the milk mixture over the dry, then immediately pour over the boiling water and whisk until smooth and combined. Add a little more red food dye at this point, if needed.

6 / Immediately pour the batter evenly into the prepared cake tins and bake for 35–40 minutes, or until a skewer inserted into the centre of a cake comes out clean. Leave to cool in the tins for 10 minutes, then run a knife around the edges and turn out onto wire racks. Peel off the baking paper and leave to cool.

7 / Make sure the cakes are cool before assembling. Stack and crumb-coat the cakes (see pages 27–28) using your chosen buttercream. Decorate simply with piped buttercream swirls and sprinkles (as pictured), OR follow one of the basic cake designs on pages 15 and 21, or the elaborate designs on pages 36, 67, 105, 138 and 159.

Apple or Pear & Elderflower Cake

This versatile cake works well with both apples and pears, so it's great to make when you have a surplus of fruit! The fruit helps to make this cake moist with bursts of fresh, fruity flavour and you have the option to simply (but effectively) decorate the outside of the cake with colourful candied dried apple or pear slices, or use this base cake recipe for a more elaborate design. If decorating with the dried fruit slices, I recommend you start dehydrating the fruit the day before you make the cake, as it needs time to dehydrate fully, then to avoid waste, reserve any fresh fruit cutoffs (which weren't used for dehydrating) to use in the cake batter later. This recipe is for 5 cake layers which, when stacked together, make a beautifully tall and elegant cake, but you can always adjust the quantities if you want to make a little bit less.

SERVES: 25–30 (MAKES: 5 X 18-CM [7-IN] CAKES)

CANDIED DRIED APPLES OR PEARS

600g [3 cups] caster or granulated sugar
800g [3½ cups] water
gel food dyes of your choice
about 4 apples or 6–9 pears (ideally these should be ripe, but not too soft)

CAKE

460g [2 cups plus 6 tsp] salted butter (or use unsalted butter and add ¾ tsp salt, or to taste), at room temperature, plus extra for greasing
540g [2¾ cups minus 2 tsp] caster or granulated sugar, plus 5 Tbsp extra for sprinkling
8 medium eggs
5 Tbsp elderflower syrup
1 Tbsp vanilla bean paste
560g [4⅓ cups] plain [all-purpose] flour (or use gluten-free flour plus 2 tsp xanthan gum)
4 tsp baking powder (use gluten-free baking powder if making gluten free – a lot of standard baking powders contain gluten)
120g [½ cup] whole yogurt
700g [1½lb] baking apples or pears (about 5–8), peeled and cored and cut into 1-cm [½-in] cubes

PLUS

1 quantity of American Buttercream (page 31) or Italian Meringue Buttercream (page 32)

1 / Make the candied dried apples or pears the day before you would like to make the cake. Preheat the oven to 75°C [167°F/Gas mark ¼] and line a baking sheet with baking paper. Put the sugar and water into a large pan and heat over a high heat until the sugar has dissolved. Add a tiny dot of gel food dye to the water.

2 / Slice the apples or pears as thinly as you can (you can do this by hand, or use a mandoline if you have one). If decorating the cake using pears, try to cut and use the centre pieces as these will all be equal in height. You can get about 3–4 pieces from the centre of each pear, whereas you can get more equal slices from the apples. You can still dehydrate the remaining fruit, or plan to use them in the cake!

3 / Add the fruit slices to the sugar mixture, then reduce the heat to medium and simmer for 10 minutes. Use a slotted spoon to remove the fruit and place them in a single layer on the lined baking sheet. Dehydrate in the oven, flipping them over after about 1½ hours. It will take at least 3 hours or more for the slices to fully dry. The finished slices will be dry and firm, but still slightly flexible and tacky from the sugar. Set aside.

Tip: For a gradient of different coloured slices, simmer the slices in batches, adding a little more food dye to the water and sugar mixture each time, starting with a lighter coloured food dye, then adding a little of a darker dye for the later batches.

4 / For the cake, preheat the oven to 180°C [350°F/ Gas mark 4]. Grease 5 x 18-cm [7-in] cake tins with butter and line the bases with baking paper.

5 / Place the butter and 540g [2¾ cups minus 2 tsp] sugar in a stand mixer (or use a handheld electric whisk) fitted with a balloon whisk attachment and whisk on high speed until fluffy and very light in colour. You can't overbeat this.

6 / Add the eggs, one at a time, beating well after each addition. Add the elderflower syrup and vanilla and beat again. The mixture will look curdled or grainy at the moment, but that's fine.

7 / Add the flour (or gluten-free flour plus xanthan gum) and baking powder and mix on slow speed or by hand until just combined. Add the yogurt and chopped apples or pears and fold in gently by hand until they are distributed through the batter – stop mixing as soon as they are. The batter will be thick.

8 / Divide the batter equally between the prepared tins and sprinkle 1 Tbsp of the extra sugar on the top of each. Bake for about 40 minutes, or until springy on top and a skewer inserted into the centre of a cake comes out mostly clean. It may have some wet apple clinging to it, but there should be no uncooked cake batter.

9 / Leave the cakes to cool in the tins for 10 minutes, then run a knife around the edges and turn out onto a wire rack. Peel off the baking paper and leave to cool completely.

10 / Make sure the cakes are cool before assembling. Stack and crumb-coat the cakes (see pages 27–28) using your chosen buttercream. Decorate simply with the candied dried apples or pears by pressing them onto the outside of your cake OR follow one of the basic cake designs on pages 15 and 18, or the elaborate designs on 36, 67, 105, 138 and 159.

"You are amazing to the core."

Vegan Vanilla Cake

SERVES: 25–30 (MAKES: 5 X 18-CM [7-IN] CAKE LAYERS)

WET INGREDIENTS
vegan butter, for greasing
1½ Tbsp white wine
   vinegar
700ml [3 cups] soy milk
280ml [1¼ cups minus
   4 tsp] sunflower oil or
   other neutral-tasting oil
1 tsp liquid from can of
   chickpeas (aquafaba)
1 Tbsp vanilla bean paste

DRY INGREDIENTS
½ tsp salt
625g [4½ cups plus 2 Tbsp]
   self-raising [self-rising]
   flour
450g [2¼ cups] caster or
   granulated sugar
2¼ Tbsp baking powder

PLUS
1 quantity of vegan
   American Buttercream
   (page 31) or vegan
   Italian Meringue
   Buttercream (page 32)
OR fresh whipped vegan
   cream and fruit

1 / Preheat the oven to 170°C [340°F/Gas mark 3]. Grease 5 x 18-cm [7-in] cake tins with vegan butter and line the bases with baking paper.

2 / In a large bowl, mix the vinegar with the soy milk until it curdles and thickens. Add the rest of the wet ingredients and the salt and stir together.

3 / In a separate large bowl, combine all the dry ingredients. Add the dry ingredients to the wet and whisk until just combined. Pour immediately into the prepared tins and bake for 25–30 minutes until springy on top and a skewer or a knife inserted into the centre comes out clean.

4 / When the cakes are baked, leave them to cool in their tins for 5 minutes, then run a knife around the edges and turn out onto wire racks. Peel off the baking paper and leave to cool.

5 / Make sure the cakes are cool before assembling. Stack and crumb-coat the cakes (see pages 27–28) using your chosen buttercream. You can can make 1 tall stacked cake or 2 shorter cakes. Follow one of the basic cake designs on pages 15, 18 and 21, or the elaborate designs on 36, 67, 105, 127, 138, 159 and 163. OR decorate simply with fresh vegan cream and fruit between the layers.

Vegan Ginger Cake

SERVES: 20–25 (MAKES 4 X 18-CM [7-IN] CAKES)

CAKE
vegan butter, for greasing
720ml [3 cups] soy milk
105g [½ cup plus 1 tsp] caster or granulated sugar
80g [⅓ cup] black treacle [molasses]
500g [2½ cups] dark muscovado [soft brown] sugar
300ml [1¼ cups] sunflower oil (or other neutral-tasting oil)
1 tsp salt
1 Tbsp vanilla bean paste
3½ tsp white wine vinegar
665g [5 cups plus 1 tsp] self-raising [self-rising] flour
2¼ Tbsp baking powder
5 Tbsp ground ginger
1¼ Tbsp ground cinnamon
130g [¾ cup plus 2 tsp] crystallized stem [candied preserved] ginger, chopped

SALTED CARAMEL
90ml [6 Tbsp] water
240g [1¼ cups plus 2 tsp] caster or granulated sugar
225ml [1 cup minus 1 Tbsp] coconut milk
fine table salt, to taste

PLUS
½ quantity of vegan Dulce de Leche Buttercream (page 33)
120g [1 cup plus 1 tsp] pecans, lightly toasted and roughly chopped

1 / Preheat the oven to 170°C [344°F/Gas mark 3] and grease 4 x 18-cm [7-in] cake tins with vegan butter and line the bases with baking paper.

2 / Place the soy milk, caster sugar, treacle, dark brown sugar, oil and salt into a pan and stir over a medium heat until the treacle has combined with the rest of the mixture. Remove from the heat and add the vanilla and vinegar.

3 / In a separate large bowl, combine all the dry ingredients together including the crystallized ginger.

4 / Add the dry ingredients to the wet ingredients and whisk until just combined. Immediately pour into the prepared tins and bake for 25–30 minutes until springy on top and a knife inserted into the centre comes out clean.

5 / Meanwhile, make the salted caramel (see page 67, without the red dye). Cover with plastic wrap and freeze for 30–45 minutes. It will thicken as it cools.

6 / When the cakes are baked, leave them to cool in their tins for 5 minutes, then run a knife around the edges and turn out onto wire racks. Peel off the baking paper and leave to cool.

7 / Ensure the cakes are cool before assembling. Stack them using the guide on page 27; in between each layer, pipe an even layer of buttercream, drizzle with salted caramel and sprinkle with pecans. Pipe more buttercream on top OR follow one of the basic cake designs on pages 15, 18 and 21, or the elaborate designs on 36, 67, 105, 138 and 159. If crumb-coating, ensure you use a dam (page 27) to help contain the caramel on each layer.

Vegan Chocolate Cake

SERVES: 20–25 (MAKES: 4 X 18-CM [7-IN] CAKES)

210ml [¾ cup plus 2 Tbsp] vegetable oil, plus extra for oiling
435ml [2 cups minus 3 Tbsp] soy milk
2¼ Tbsp white wine vinegar
435g [3⅓ cups] plain [all-purpose] flour
150g [1½ cups] unsweetened cocoa powder, sifted

3½ tsp baking powder
585g [3 cups minus 1 Tbsp] caster or granulated sugar
1 tsp salt
1 Tbsp vanilla bean paste
1 Tbsp instant coffee granules (optional)
270ml [1 cup plus 2 Tbsp] boiling water

1 / 1 Preheat the oven to 180°C [350°F/Gas mark 4]. Oil 4 x 18-cm [7-in] cake tins and line the bases with a circle of baking paper.

2 / Pour the soy milk into a large bowl, add the vinegar and stir. The mixture should curdle a little. Set aside for now.

3 / Place the flour, sifted cocoa powder, baking powder and sugar in a separate large bowl and whisk to quickly combine.

4 / Return to the soy milk mixture and add the oil, salt and vanilla and whisk quickly. The oil will remain separated, but that's OK.

5 / Put the coffee granules (if using) into a heatproof bowl and pour in the boiling water. Stir and set aside.

6 / Pour the milk mixture over the dry ingredients, then immediately add the hot coffee and whisk until smooth and combined. Divide the batter between the prepared cake tins and bake for 30–35 minutes until a skewer inserted into the cente of a cake comes out clean.

7 / Leave the cakes to cool in the tins for 10 minutes, then transfer to a wire rack, peel off the baking paper and leave to cool completely.

8 / Make sure the cakes are cool before assembling. Stack and crumb-coat the cakes using the guide on pages 27–28. You can can make 1 tall stacked cake or 2 shorter cakes OR follow one of the basic cake designs on pages 15, 18 and 21, or the elaborate designs on 36, 67, 105, 124, 138, 159 and 184.

Vegan Red Velvet Cake

SERVES: 20–25 (MAKES: 4 X 18-CM [7-IN] CAKES)

vegan butter, for greasing
435ml [2 cups minus 3 Tbsp] soy milk
2½ Tbsp white wine vinegar
550g [4¼ cups] plain [all-purpose] flour
1½ Tbsp unsweetened cocoa powder, sifted
3 tsp baking powder

585g [3 cups minus 1 Tbsp] caster or granulated sugar
210ml [1 cup minus 2 Tbsp] sunflower oil (or other neutral-tasting oil)
1 tsp salt
1 Tbsp vanilla bean paste
red gel food dye
270ml [1¼ cups minus 2 Tbsp] boiling water

PLUS
1 quantity of vegan American Buttercream (page 31) or vegan Italian Meringue Buttercream (page 32)

1 / Preheat the oven to 180°C [350°F/Gas mark 4]. Grease the base and sides of 4 x 18-cm [7-in] cake tins with vegan butter and line the bases with circles of baking paper.

2 / Add the soy milk to a large bowl, then add the vinegar and stir. The mixture should curdle a little. Set aside for now.

3 / In a separate large bowl, add the flour, sifted cocoa powder, baking powder and sugar and whisk to quickly combine.

4 / Return to the soy milk mixture. Add the oil, salt and vanilla bean paste and whisk quickly. The oil will remain separated, but that's fine. Add red food dye to colour a deep red.

5 / Pour the milk mixture over the dry ingredients, then immediately pour over the boiling water and whisk until smooth and combined. Add a little more red food dye at this point, if needed. Pour the batter between the prepared cake tins and bake for 30–35 minutes until a skewer or knife inserted into the centre of a cake comes out clean.

6 / Leave the cakes to cool in the tins for 10 minutes, before running a knife around the edges and turning out onto wire racks. Peel off the paper and leave to cool.

7 / Make sure the cakes are cool before assembling. Stack and crumb-coat the cakes using the guide on pages 27–28. Decorate simply with piped buttercream, swirls and sprinkles, OR follow one of the basic cake designs on pages 15, 18 and 21, or the elaborate designs on 36, 67, 105, 138 and 159.

Cake Making & Decorating Tips

LEVELLING

Sometimes your cake might dome in the middle, which is not ideal for stacking. Level your cakes by using a serrated knife and judging by eye, or use a cake leveller. It is much easier if you wrap it tightly in plastic wrap and chill it in the freezer before levelling.

ASSEMBLING CAKE LAYERS

First, you want to use a cake board that is just slightly larger than your cakes. Put a blob of your frosting on the cake board, then place the first cake layer on top. The frosting will stop it sliding about! Cover the top of the cake with a solid layer of room-temperature buttercream (thickness comes down to personal preference but you don't want 2.5-cm [1-in] thick frosting!). You can pipe this buttercream on, or you can just spread it on with an offset spatula. If using jam and or curd, see the 'dam' technique

below. Place the second cake layer of cake on top. If you're planning on covering the sides of the cake, it can be helpful if the buttercream squeezes out of the side of the cake a little bit. Repeat until the last cake layer is placed on top.

DAM

This is useful when you are working with softer fillings in between cake layers, like jam or curd. You pipe a 'dam' of buttercream (see picture below) around the circumference of the cake so that it can be filled with the softer filling, which then won't ooze out.

STACKING MULTIPLE TIERS

When stacking a cake with different sizes of tier ensure that each tier has a cake board underneath; use thinner cake boards for the tiers higher up. Also, make sure each tier is properly chilled before

stacking. If carving into a tiered cake (like the Wedding Korovai 'Kitovai' cake on page 108), cut your cake boards so that each one is recessed back a bit. For 3 or more tiers or softer, more fragile cakes, it helps to use dowels or thick straws. Place the dowels or thick straws in the bottom and middle cake tiers. Insert 3–5 (more for the bottom tier) down into the cake until it reaches the base, then trim the tops so they are completely level with the cake. It helps to mark the straw or dowel where it needs to be cut, by pulling it back out a bit, then cutting it and pushing it back into place. The dowels – rather than the actual cake – should take the weight of the tiers above.

Tip: When stacking cakes, brush each layer with Simple Syrup (page 33) to moisten them and prevent them drying out. You can also use Simple Syrup when the cakes are still warm from the oven.

CRUMB COATING
This is the first coat of buttercream you apply all over your cake in order to stop the pesky crumbs sneaking into your second layer, and so that you can play about with colour on your second layer. Chill your crumb-coated cake in the fridge or freezer, before applying the finishing coat.

To crumb-coat your cake layers, smooth buttercream all over the tops and sides of the cake using an offset spatula. Then, to get this as smooth as possible, it helps to use a turntable and cake scraper (see picture below). Hold the scraper at a 45-degree angle and slowly spin the turntable to get a smooth finish. You may have to do this a couple of times.

If you are working on a cake that doesn't have too many crumbs when you coat it, then it is sometimes effective to leave it as a 'semi-naked' cake, which has some of the cake peaking out through the buttercream and can look very elegant. To get an even finish on this, warm the cake scraper that you are using by running it under hot water – the heat helps make everything nice and smooth.

To smooth the top, use an offset spatula to smooth the rough edges inwards. Again, use a warm offset spatula to get an even finish on this. Alternatively, you can use a sharp knife to simply cut off the buttercream edges. Sometimes it can look effective to leave the top edges rough and uneven (see the Crème Brûlée Cake on page 17), especially if this contrasts with a neat and smooth design elsewhere.

FINISHING THE BUTTERCREAM COAT IN FUN WAYS

This is the best part because you can play around with COLOUR!! The crumb coat should now be properly chilled and firm, so you can apply colour and texture without disturbing it. Think of it like a blank canvas, and the second coat as art.

If you add a few blobs of colour and smooth with the cake scraper, you can achieve a watercolour effect.

Alternatively, you can play with texture: apply different colours using an offset spatula. Smooth some bits, and allow the texture to show through on others (see the Holi cake on page 172).

You can also paint with buttercream using a palette knife almost like an oil painting.

To create a distinct line between two different colours of buttercream (see the Day of the Dead cake on page 159), first use a knife to mark a diagonal line in the buttercream on the crumb-coated cake as a guide. Then use a palette knife to spread one colour of buttercream on one side of the marked line (best to start with the darker colour). Smooth as normal, then repeat with the second colour of buttercream on the other side. This time cover the previously applied buttercream with baking paper, ensuring it lines right up to the edge (see picture above). It will prevent buttercream from going beyond the line of the baking paper.

USING CAKE FLOUR

If you live in the US, using 'cake flour' instead of plain [all-purpose] flour will make your cakes softer, lighter and more tender as it has less protein. In the UK you can buy 'cake and pastry flour' for the same results.

CAKE STRIPS

To bake your cakes more evenly, so they rise higher and there's less doming, you can use 'cake strips'. To make your own, cut an old tea towel [dish towel] into strips, soak in water and squeeze out the excess. Tie the strips around your cake tins using a clip to hold them together, then fill your tins with the cake batter and bake according to the recipe (you may need to add a few extra minutes' baking time). You can also buy purpose-made cake strips. This trick also ensures that the sides of the cake don't brown as much. Normally the outside of a cake bakes the fastest, so it ends up being more cooked than the centre.

FREEZING CAKES

Most cakes freeze very well, just wrap them tightly in plastic wrap first. The freezer keeps them moist and sometimes makes them taste even better! Avoid putting cakes into the fridge unless they are already covered with buttercream (this will help lock in the moisture), as the fridge dries cakes out.

GLUTEN-FREE SUBSTITUTION NOTES

There are gluten-free substitutions throughout the book that call for gluten-free flour plus xanthan gum. Some gluten-free flour blends already contain xanthan gum, so check the pack and omit it if your blend does! Different flour blends will taste a little different, so find one you like and that works for you. Many baking powders also contain gluten, so find a gluten-free baking powder (which works just as well) if you need your recipe to be entirely gluten free.

FOOD DYES

I use gel food dyes throughout this book and oil-based gel food dyes if colouring pure chocolate or candy melts (the small amount of water in water-based food dyes will cause it to seize). Gel food dye is ideal as it is more concentrated, so less likely to affect the consistencies of icing, buttercream, meringue, etc. BUT the quality of different gel food dye brands varies, e.g. some supermarket brands can lack pigment and don't stay vibrant after baking! Make sure to find a good brand that you can trust. You can also use oil-based gel food dyes to colour buttercream – I find that it tends to mix better with the butter and helps provide a vibrant colour with less food dye.

MAKING SHAPES FROM RICE PAPER WRAPPERS

Fill a large shallow dish (wide enough so that the wrapper can be dipped straight in) with warm water. Soak a rice paper spring roll wrapper in the water for 1 minute, then place on baking paper, a silicone mat or a rolling pin in whatever shape you would like them to set into. You can use clips to roll up or create folds in the paper or mat. If you would like to add a colour, add food dye to the water and create different baths for different colours. You can also mix food dye with water and paint or flick onto the shapes. Leave to dry overnight.

Buttercreams

American Buttercream

These buttercream recipes make a large quantity so need a stand mixer! If working with a handheld electric whisk, divide it into 2 batches to make it easier.

Your classic sweet and easy-to-make buttercream. This recipe makes a large quantity, enough to fill and crumb-coat all of the tiered cake recipes. There should also be leftovers for the second buttercream coat. Halve this quantity if you are not covering the top and sides of the cake. You can make three-quarters of this recipe if you are just crumb-coating your cake. You can also make a third extra if you want to make the biggest batch possible in one go (if decorating multiple cakes). This amount will still fit in a stand mixer bowl, but avoid making a larger quantity if you don't want the mixture spilling over the sides! This recipe is quick and easy to make which is helpful when you're in a rush!

MAKES: ENOUGH TO FILL, CRUMB-COAT AND COVER A TIERED CAKE

550g [2½ cups] unsalted butter, at room temperature
salt, to taste (this adds a depth of flavour to the sweetness and helps to bring out flavour! I also often use salted butter, but if you like a less salty buttercream, add the salt yourself)
800g [5¾ cups] icing [confectioners'] sugar
milk, to thin

OPTIONAL FLAVOURINGS
vanilla extract, rose water, orange or lemon zest, raspberry powder, coffee, almond extract

1 / Place the butter, salt and icing sugar in a stand mixer (or use a handheld electric whisk) fitted with a balloon whisk attachment and whisk on slow speed until the icing sugar is combined (you may want to cover the bowl with a tea towel [dish towel] to prevent the icing sugar flying everywhere!).

2 / Increase the speed to high and whisk until light and fluffy, scraping down the sides of the bowl with a spatula when necessary to ensure everything mixes properly. Add milk, 1 Tbsp at a time, to achieve a spreadable consistency. Now add any flavourings.

3 / If not using straightaway, cover with plastic wrap. Refrigerate if not using for a few days; it should be fine for 2–3 days at room temperature. If refrigerating, let it come back to room temperature and whisk before using to make it easier to work with.

Vegan tip: To make this vegan, you can use a good-quality vegan butter that is at least 75% fat content. Don't try to use a vegan butter with less fat content, as it will be very soft at room temperature and difficult to work with. If your butter is 70% fat minimum, you can help it structurally by using half vegetable shortening, although play about with the ratios to see what works for you. Some people use 100% shortening, but I personally avoid shortening. If you're using shortening, this can become grainy when overwhipped (unlike butter), so only add it after you've creamed together the vegan butter and icing sugar, then whisk until combined again. You don't need to add any plant-based milk to achieve a good consistency when using vegan butter or 100% shortening based buttercream.

Italian Meringue Buttercream

See the American Buttercream recipe on the previous page for advice about the quantities this makes, and when to scale it up or down. It helps to have a stand mixer for this buttercream, as you will need to be whisking the egg whites and adding the sugar while also keeping an eye on the temperature of the sugar syrup. This buttercream is silky smooth and less sweet than American Buttercream. It is so easy to work with and sets very firm in the fridge, so when you slice the cake, the layers of buttercream will be very distinct. This is my preferred option for tiered cakes – it just takes a little more time to make but is so worth it.

MAKES: ENOUGH TO FILL, CRUMB-COAT AND COVER A TIERED CAKE

225g [8oz] egg whites (from about 7–8 medium eggs)
560g [2¾ cups] caster or granulated sugar
pinch of salt

225ml [1 cup minus 1 Tbsp] water
½ tsp cream of tartar
675g [3 cups] unsalted butter, at room temperature

OPTIONAL FLAVOURINGS
vanilla extract, rose water, orange or lemon zest, raspberry powder, coffee, almond extract

1 / Put the egg whites into a stand mixer fitted with a balloon whisk attachment (or use a handheld electric whisk). Add half the sugar to a separate bowl.

2 / Put the remaining sugar, the salt and water into a pan and place over a medium-high heat, stirring occasionally to dissolve all the sugar. Once the mixture starts bubbling, don't stir, and immediately start whisking the egg whites in the stand mixer. Add the cream of tartar once it is frothy, then when it reaches soft peaks, start adding the sugar, 1 Tbsp at a time, until thick and shiny. You will need to time this with the sugar syrup reaching 115°C [239°F]. If necessary, slow down the mixer (but don't stop it) or reduce the heat for the sugar syrup. When all the sugar has been added to the meringue and the syrup has reached 115°C [239°F], pour the syrup in a thin stream down the side of the mixer, mixing on maximum speed. Do not slow the mixer, or pour the syrup directly onto the whisk, as it may splash and it is very hot. Leave to whisk on high speed (to cool the meringue faster) for 30 minutes, or until the bottom of the bowl feels room temperature; there is so much sugar in the meringue that you won't overbeat it.

3 / Now add the butter, 3–4 cubes at a time, beating well after each addition. Continue until all the butter has been added. The mixture will go from firm to becoming more liquid, and this is normal – just keep adding more butter. When you have added all the butter, the mixture will return to being fluffy and the perfect consistency for spreading. At this point you can add flavourings. Use right away, or cover with plastic wrap if using later in the day.

Tip: If the buttercream is left out too long, you may find the fat separating slightly when spreading onto cakes. To fix this, just remove about an eighth of the mixture and microwave until slightly melted at the sides. Add this back to the main mixture and stir quickly with a spatula until incorporated and back to being silky and smooth.

Tip: You can refrigerate the buttercream for up to a week. When you remove it from the fridge, it will be very hard like a block of butter, so you will need to soften it by heating it in the microwave in 15-second bursts. Be patient and make sure that the butter does not melt. If the butter does melt, pop it back in the fridge to firm. When you have brought the buttercream to room temperature, it still won't look right, but that is fine. Transfer it to a stand mixer (or use a handheld electric whisk) and whisk on high speed until smooth and creamy again. Be patient; if it's not coming together it either needs whisking longer or bringing to the correct temperature.

Dulce de Leche Buttercream

This buttercream has an incredible caramel flavour that really complements warming spices, fruit and chocolate: it is delicious with the Apple or Pear & Elderflower Cake (page 21), Chocolate Cake (page 14) and Ginger Cake (page 13).

Note: This naturally has a deeper golden colour than American or Italian meringue buttercream, so avoid it if you want a vibrantly coloured buttercream.

MAKES: ENOUGH TO FILL, CRUMB-COAT AND COVER A TIERED CAKE

600g [2⅔ cups] salted butter, at room temperature (see Vegan Tip on page 31)

720g [2⅓ cups] canned dulce de leche (or use vegan dulce de leche)

1 / Place the butter in a stand mixer (or use a handheld electric whisk) fitted with a balloon whisk attachment and whisk on high until light and fluffy, scraping down the sides of the bowl with a spatula when necessary.

2 / Add half of the dulce de leche and whisk until just combined. Add the remaining dulce de leche and whisk again until just combined. Be cautious, as this buttercream can be easily overwhipped! For best results, use immediately. You can also refrigerate this buttercream; just bring it back to room temperature before using.

Simple Syrup

For all cake recipes, this simple syrup helps to keep your cakes moist and delicious. Make a big batch and store it in an airtight container in the fridge for up to a month. You can also store it in a squeezy bottle to make it easier to pour onto your cakes. This is a plain syrup (no flavour added), but you can easily add your own favourite flavours – vanilla (after boiling) and citrus rinds work very well.

200g [1 cup] caster or granulated sugar
240ml [1 cup] water

1 / Place the sugar and water in a pan and bring to the boil for 2 minutes, stirring constantly until the sugar has dissolved. Leave to cool, then transfer to an airtight container or squeezy bottle. Easy!

Birthdays

Granite Nature Cake

This is the perfect birthday cake for nature and magic lovers. As with many of the cakes, feel free to get creative and use your favourite colours to make this one of a kind. For enjoyable and relaxing decorating, it's best to make the cake and decorations the day before (also the rice paper wrapper decorations need to be left to dry out overnight anyway), then make the buttercream, stack and decorate the following day.

SERVES: 20–30 (DEPENDING ON THE CAKE YOU HAVE CHOSEN TO MAKE)

GREEN CAKE MOSS
1 egg
15g [2½ tsp] golden syrup [light corn syrup] (or honey)
30g [2½ Tbsp] caster or granulated sugar
green food dye
30g [3⅔ Tbsp] plain [all-purpose] flour
½ tsp baking powder

PLUS
rice paper spring roll wrappers
edible gold paint
edible wafer paper

choose 1 cake recipe (see pages 10–26), such as the Apple or Pear & Elderflower Cake (page 21) or the Ginger Cake (page 13), baked and cooled
1 quantity of American Buttercream (page 31) or Italian Meringue Buttercream (page 32)
green, brown, pink, orange, purple, black and white food dyes
edible gold leaf
edible flowers
1 quantity of Candied Dried Apples (page 21)

1 / For the green cake moss, whisk the egg, golden syrup and sugar together in a large bowl until light in colour and very foamy. Add green food dye until the desired colour is achieved. Sift in the flour and baking powder and fold in gently. Fill a mug a third of the way up with the batter and microwave for 45–55 seconds until the cake isn't sinking back down when you remove it from the microwave. Use a fork to remove the cake from the mug and leave to partially cool before tearing into pieces.

2 / For the rice paper spring roll shapes, follow the instructions on page 30. Leave to dry overnight. Once dry, you can paint some of the edges and folds with a little edible gold paint.

Note: The rice paper spring roll wrappers are different to wafer paper, as they are hard and go soft after soaking. They are less fragile after soaking and have a translucent look to them, which is ideal for making large sail shapes. You can also cut them before soaking to get different-sized sails.

3 / To make the wafer paper mushrooms, cut the wafer paper into circles to fit into a 4-cm [1½-in] silicone semisphere mould. The paper will just break unless you wet it, so dampen it with a little water using a paintbrush. Wait a few seconds until it becomes flexible and shape it into the silicone moulds. As with the rice paper sails, you can experiment with adding different colours by painting or flicking on. Just use a

lot less water with these, as when they get too wet they are prone to tearing and become difficult to handle. To make the stems, just cut the wafer paper into a long rectangle, then wet in the same way and roll up into a stem shape. Leave to dry overnight. Once dry, you can paint some of the edges and folds with a little edible gold paint.

Note: Wafer paper looks like paper, but is edible. You can buy it in different colours, but white is perfect as you can add food dye to colour it however you wish.

4 / Make sure the cakes are cool before assembling. Stack and crumb-coat the cakes (see pages 27–28). Colour 500–550g [17–19oz] of the buttercream green, then spread a layer of green buttercream all over the chilled crumb-coated cake using a palette knife and smooth again. You don't need to completely cover the white crumb coat – some marbling is nice! Refrigerate until firm again.

5 / Cut a large piece of baking paper that is just taller than the top of the cake and create a diagonal edge on it so that when placed against the cake, you still see some of the green buttercream

underneath. Divide the remaining uncoloured buttercream between 6 bowls. Add different gel colour food dyes to each of these (brown, pink, orange, purple, white and black). Add a little black food dye to each as well to make these colours earthier, and roughly mix each bowl, leaving swirls of food dye as this is what will create the marbling effect later. Randomly spoon the different coloured buttercream onto the baking paper (you can peek underneath to see what the reverse will look like on the actual cake), then smooth out with a palette knife so that it's an even layer. Lift and place against the chilled cake, then use a fondant smoothing tool just to even out any kinks in the paper (although don't worry too much as it looks good to have some roughness!), and ensure the buttercream is stuck on to the cake.

6 / Chill in the freezer (or fridge, although this will take longer) until the buttercream is completely firm, then peel off the baking paper, revealing your marbled buttercream. Apply lines of gold paint within the marbling. Decorate however your creativity takes you, using the edible gold leaf and flowers, candied apple slices, cake moss, sails and mushrooms.

STEP 5 ▼

Edible Cat Terrarium

You can customize this cake and turn it into the recipient's dream landscape! It could be purely plant life, it could contain any animals you like, and you could even put in miniature people. If you're not confident icing cookies, you could use plastic or paper figures, or even make creatures out of fondant. Play about with the design and turn it into the perfect birthday cake! For the optimum level of relaxation when making this, I recommend making the decorations, iced cookies, mousse and cake the day before, then on the day just have fun adding in the cake and decorations. The edible kohakutou (Japanese candy) rocks are optional. Although they are actually very quick to make, they take a long time to form a crunchy sugary crust. Once they have hardened, they are great to store in a jar and use to decorate other baked creations, or just to snack on.

Can be made vegan!

SERVES: ABOUT 8 (MAKES 1 LARGE TERRARIUM, OR YOU CAN MAKE MINI INDIVIDUAL TERRARIUMS!)

KOHAKUTOU JELLY ROCKS
150ml [⅔ cup minus 2 tsp] water
140g [¾ cup minus 2 tsp] caster or granulated sugar
2g [1 tsp] agar agar powder
food dyes of choice

DECORATED ALPACA, DINOSAUR AND CAT COOKIES
1 quantity of Ginger and Orange Cookie dough (page 94)
1 quantity of Royal Icing (page 94)
food dyes of choice

CHOCOLATE MOUSSE
EITHER see page 87 (will make lots extra, but the remainder can be served in cups. Alternatively, you could make ½ this recipe)
OR for vegan chocolate mousse:
120g [½ cup] coconut milk (just the thick cream scooped off the top)
200g [1¼ cups plus 1 Tbsp] dark [bittersweet] chocolate (at least 70% cooca solids), finely chopped
1 tsp vanilla bean paste
120ml [½ cup] aquafaba (liquid from can of chickpeas)
¼ tsp cream of tartar
50g [¼ cup] caster or granulated sugar

CHOCOLATE CAKE
½ quantity of Chocolate Cake (page 14) or Vegan Chocolate Cake (page 25) (this makes a little bit extra but it's easy to put to good use...)

GREEN 'MOSS'
6–7 pale-coloured cookies (such as Rich Tea) or shortbread
green food dye or 1 tsp matcha powder

PLUS
about 150g [5oz] different coloured fondant of your choice
1 raspberry
edible sugar rocks

Note: The kohakutou jelly rocks take several days to form a hard crust, so ideally they need to be made well in advance. If you don't have the time to make these, you can just use store-bought edible rocks which also look great.

"There are more people rooting for you than you realize."

1 / First, make the jelly rocks (optional). Place the water, sugar and agar agar powder in a pan and heat over a medium heat, stirring intermittently, until the agar agar and sugar have dissolved. Increase the heat to high and cook until the mixture is bubbling. Continue bubbling for 3 minutes.

2 / Remove from the heat and pour into a wide, shallow dish. Immediately use a cocktail stick [toothpick] to add blobs of food dye. You can use multiple colours. Spread and swirl the food dye through the mixture, then chill in the fridge for 30 minutes, or until completely set, although it will also set at room temperature.

3 / Once set, run a knife around the edges, then turn out onto a chopping board. Use a knife to carve the jelly into rock (or crystal) shapes, then place on baking paper and leave at room temperature exposed to the air. In a couple of days, the jelly will become hard and crunchy on the outside. At this point, turn them over so that the other side is exposed to the air and leave to dry out on the outside again for another couple of days. Once hardened and crystallized, they are ready to use!

4 / Next, make the decorated cookies. Take the Ginger and Orange cookie dough, roll it out and cut out using different cutters, then bake, cool and decorate the cooled cookies using royal icing (page 94). Leave to set for at least 4 hours, or preferably overnight (setting time depends on humidity).

5 / Next, make the chocolate mousse following the instructions on page 87. Or, if making vegan, place the coconut cream, chocolate and vanilla in a heatproof bowl set over a pan of simmering water, making sure the base of the bowl doesn't touch the water, and stir until the chocolate has melted and the mixture is smooth and combined. Set aside to cool.

6 / When the ganache has cooled to room temperature, pour the aquafaba into a stand mixer (or use a handheld electric whisk) fitted with the balloon whisk attachment and whisk on high speed until frothy. Add the cream of tartar and whisk again. Add the sugar, 1 Tbsp at a time, whisking well after each addition. Continue until all the sugar has been added and the mixture has reached stiff peaks.

7 / Add a quarter of the aquafaba to the ganache and fold in until combined. Add the rest of the aquafaba in 2 more batches, gently folding in after each addition to avoid knocking out too much air. The mousse will deflate a little, but you don't want it to be completely flat!

8 / Pour the mousse into a glass bowl you want to serve your dessert in. Or you can divide it between smaller glass jars for individual portions. Place in the fridge and leave for at least 5 hours until set.

9 / Meanwhile, make and bake the chocolate cake following the instructions on page 14 or 25.

10 / While the cake is cooling, make the plants using fondant. You can use plunger cutters to stamp out ascending sizes of the same shaped flower, then stack them together and curve the edges upwards to make a succulent shape. You can also cut various shapes out to create some taller plants. To make the raspberry mushroom, just arrange it on top of a piece of fondant for the mushroom base. You can also use meringue instead of fondant, but unless you need to make a whole batch of meringue for something else, it's more convenient to use fondant!

11 / When the cake is cool, break it into pieces and arrange larger cake pieces and crumbled cake on top of the chilled mousse to create a landscape.

12 / To create the green 'moss', crush the cookies in a food processor or place in a bag and bash with a rolling pin, then add matcha powder or a blob of green food dye to colour green. Seal the bag again and shake if using matcha, or if using food dye use your fingers on the outside of the bag to rub the food dye evenly throughout.

13 / For the final decorating touches, sprinkle the green cookie crumbs over the cake, then decorate further with edible rocks, the edible jelly rocks (if using), fondant plants, raspberry mushroom and animal cookies.

Dinosaur Burnt Basque Cheesecake

Spanish burnt Basque cheesecake is one recipe that can't go wrong, and the cloud-like custardy interior combined with the caramelized crust (yes it's 'burnt' on purpose though it doesn't actually taste burnt – it is just deeply caramelized) makes it irresistible. It took a little while to think of a way to decorate this while still embracing its charming ruggedness, so here we are – a volcanic dinosaur landscape. The cheesecake itself takes minutes to mix up, and you can make your own dinosaur cookies or buy some, or even use some dinosaur figurines!

SERVES: 8–10 (MAKES 1 X 18-CM [7-IN] CHEESECAKE)

DINOSAUR COOKIES
1 quantity of Ginger and Orange Cookie dough (page 94)

CHEESECAKE
butter or oil, for greasing
170g [¾ cup plus 1½ Tbsp] caster or granulated sugar

460g [2 cups plus 2 tsp] whole cream cheese
3 medium eggs
240ml [1 cup] double [heavy] cream
½ tsp salt
2 tsp vanilla bean paste
25g [2 Tbsp] plain [all-purpose] flour (or use 20g [¼ cup minus 1 tsp]

cornflour [cornstarch] to make gluten free)

PLUS
¼ quantity of Royal Icing (page 94)
yellow, orange and red gel food dyes

1 / Roll out the Ginger and Orange cookie dough and cut out using dinosaur cutters, then bake and cool (see page 94). You will have more cookies than you need but the extras can be enjoyed as they are! Decorate the cooled cookies using royal icing. Leave to set for at least 4 hours, or preferably overnight (setting time depends on humidity).

2 / When ready to bake the cheesecake, preheat the oven to 200°C [400°F/Gas mark 6]. Grease a 20-cm [8-in] cake tin and line the base and sides with baking paper, allowing 5cm [2in] of overhang above the top of the tin. You will need to press the paper into the sides, so it will naturally crease in places.

3 / Whisk the sugar and cream cheese together in a stand mixer fitted with the balloon whisk attachment (or use a handheld electric whisk) until smooth. Add the eggs, 1 at a time, whisking well after each

addition. Add the cream, salt and vanilla and whisk until combined. Sift in the flour and mix in again until everything is combined.

4 / Divide the batter between 3 bowls and dye each one a different colour: yellow, orange and red.

5 / Pour the red batter into the prepared tin, then pour the orange on top, right in the centre (it will merge as the batter is liquid, but that's fine!), and then lastly, the yellow. Bake for 40–50 minutes until deep brown on top and it is still jiggly in the centre.

6 / Leave to cool in the tin for 30 minutes, then remove and peel off the baking paper. Place in the fridge to cool completely before serving. You can serve it warm but it will have a more gooey centre.

7 / Top with the dinosaur cookies just before serving.

Kagekone

This bake has its origins in Denmark where it's made for birthday parties! Traditionally it is decorated with lots of candy, gummies, marzipans, nuts, or anything colourful to make it resemble (as much as possible when using pastry!) the person whose birthday it is. Everyone sings happy birthday and the birthday boy or girl cuts the head off the 'kagemand'/ 'kagekone' ('kagemand' is in the shape of a boy; 'kagekone' in the shape of a girl), and everyone screams! It's a great way to make a different and really fun, unforgettable birthday! Plus it's a delicious alternative to a cake, especially for people who are big pastry fans (most of us, right?). The version I've provided here is a little more complex with the decorating and piping, just to give an idea of what you could do, but this bake is accessible to everyone. The fun in this recipe is to use this as a basis to create your own 'kagemand'/ 'kagekone' design – whether you're a good decorator or not. It's great for kids to get stuck in and help decorate – buy a big variety of candy and icing, and just let them loose!

Ideally you want to make the Danish pastry for this the day before, so that the next day you can focus on cutting the shapes, baking and decorating.

SERVES: 25–30

DANISH PASTRY

(or use store-bought puff pastry. Although this isn't the same as the yeasted laminated Danish pastry, you will be able to create the same shapes. No need to let store-bought puff pastry rise before baking either, as it does not contain yeast)

375g [2⅔ cups] strong white flour

375g [2¾ cups plus 1½ Tbsp] plain [all-purpose] white flour, plus extra for dusting

15g [1 Tbsp] salt

14g [½oz] fast-action dried [active-dry] yeast

120g [⅔ cup] caster or granulated sugar

190ml [¾ cup plus 1 Tbsp] whole milk

3 medium eggs

grated zest of 1 lemon

135ml [½ cup plus 1 Tbsp] water

375g [1⅔ cups] unsalted butter

AMARETTO CRÈME PÂTISSIÈRE

130ml [½ cup plus 2 tsp] whole milk

1 tsp vanilla bean paste

2 medium egg yolks

30g [2½ Tbsp] caster or granulated sugar

10g [3½ tsp] plain [all-purpose] flour

1 tsp cornflour [cornstarch]

2 tsp amaretto

PECAN AND MAPLE FILLING

300g [2⅔ cups] pecans

100g [½ cup] dark muscovado [soft brown] sugar

3 Tbsp maple syrup

50g [3½ Tbsp] salted butter, melted

ORANGE LIQUEUR GLAZE

1 Tbsp orange liqueur

110g [¾ cup plus ½ Tbsp] icing [confectioners'] sugar

juice of ½ orange

grated zest of 1 orange

WHITE CHOCOLATE SKIRT

500g [17oz] white chocolate

pink oil-based food dye or cocoa butter

MARZIPAN

1 quantity of marzipan (page 121) or use store-bought

gel food colours

ROYAL ICING

see page 94

gel food dye

PLUS

sunflower or other neutral-tasting oil, for oiling

large punnet of raspberries, to decorate

1 egg, lightly beaten for egg wash

edible flowers

sprinkles

black edible paint or black food dye mixed with water

red edible paint or red food dye mixed with water

rose lustre dust

edible silver dust (optional)

edible gold leaf (optional)

1 / To make the Danish pastry, place the flours, salt, yeast, sugar, milk, eggs, lemon zest and water in a stand mixer fitted with the dough hook attachment. Ensure the salt and yeast aren't directly touching and mix on speed 2 until combined. Keep kneading for about 2 minutes, or until the dough feels manageable and mostly smooth. You don't need to knead it a lot as it will be worked further from being rolled out repeatedly. If you don't have a stand mixer, mix and knead by hand. Cover the dough with plastic wrap and leave to rest in the fridge for 15 minutes.

2 / Slice the butter lengthways into large thin rectangles. Place these on a piece of baking paper and fold up the edges so that you have a rectangular package of butter (about 30 x 20cm [12 x 8in]). Bash the butter with a rolling pin to soften it and form a smooth rectangle of even thickness. Chill in the fridge for about 15 minutes.

3 / Take the dough and the butter rectangle out of the fridge. Roll out the dough on a lightly floured work surface into a rectangle (twice as long as the butter rectangle, but the same width) and try to keep the edges as straight as possible. Remove the paper from the butter rectangle and place it in the centre of the dough.

4 / Do a book fold: fold both ends of the dough over the butter so that they meet in the centre, then fold in the centre so that both sides meet, like closing a book. Wrap this in plastic wrap and chill in the fridge for 25 minutes. Roll out into a rectangle again (about the same length as the first), do another book fold, wrap in plastic wrap and place in the fridge for another 25 minutes. Do one last roll and book fold and return to the fridge for 3 hours, or preferably overnight before using.

5 / For the amaretto crème pâtissière, add the milk and vanilla bean paste to a small pan and heat over a medium heat until just starting to bubble. Meanwhile, using a balloon whisk, whisk the egg yolks and sugar together in a bowl until light and fluffy. Add the flour and cornflour and mix until just combined. When the milk mixture is bubbling, pour a small amount (about a third) into the egg yolk mixture, while constantly whisking quickly, then gradually add the rest, whisking constantly. Mix until combined, then pour it all back into the saucepan.

6 / Put the pan back over a medium heat and keep whisking until the mixture is very thick. Use a silicone spatula towards the end as it starts thickening. Take the mixture off the heat and stir in the amaretto. Transfer the mixture to a bowl, cover with plastic wrap (touching the surface of the crème pat) and place in the fridge to cool.

7 / Meanwhile, prepare the pecan and maple filling. Blitz the pecans in a food processor until fine, then mix in a bowl with the sugar, maple syrup and melted butter. Set aside for now.

8 / In a separate bowl, make the orange liqueur glaze by mixing all the ingredients together. Set aside.

SHAPING THE PASTRIES
(for the pinwheels, 2 braids and a spiral head)
9 / Line 2 large baking sheets with baking paper. Remove the dough from the fridge, unwrap and cut off a third. Cover the rest with plastic wrap and place back in the fridge for now. Roll the dough on a lightly floured surface into a thin large rectangle (about 4–5mm [¼in] thick), then use a pizza wheel to cut out two 22 x 30-cm [8½ x 12-in] rectangles. These will be the 'hair braids'. Cut out 6 x 8-cm [3¼-in] squares. These will be the pinwheels at the bottom of the 'dress'.

10 / For the braids, spoon the pecan filling down the centre. Cut into the edges on either side at 1.5–2-cm [⅝–¾-in] intervals. Bring the first left-hand 'flap' over the filling, then overlap this slightly with the corresponding right-hand 'flap'. Keep alternating to create a braid all the way down. Repeat with the second braid.

11 / For the pinwheels, cut diagonal lines from all 4 corners towards the centre but leaving a gap. Bring the left-hand corners of each dough segment in to create a pinwheel (just as you would do with a paper pinwheel). Make 6 of these.

12 / Remove a quarter of the remaining dough from the fridge and roll out as before. Cut this into long thin strips (about 2cm [¾in] wide), then spread the pecan mixture on top. Wind these around to create a large spiral (about 12cm [4½in] in diameter). This will be the 'head'.

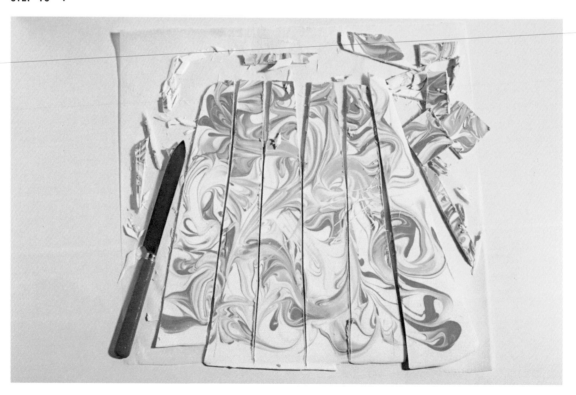

13 / Arrange these shapes on the lined baking sheet, positioning the braids next to the head so that they will attach when baking. Place the pinwheels on the baking sheet. Cover with lightly oiled plastic wrap or a proving bag and leave to rise at room temperature for 45–60 minutes.

SHAPING THE CHELSEA BUN-STYLE ROLLS

14 / Remove the remaining dough from the fridge and roll out as before into a 25 x 55-cm [10 x 21-in] rectangle. Brush with the remaining pecan filling, then roll up into a log, starting with the long edge. Pinch the seams together and slice off the end pieces. Use a sharp knife and a sawing motion to slice the dough into 21 equal-sized pieces. Arrange these on the second lined baking sheet in the shape of a dress and leave to rise at room temperature for 30–60 minutes.

15 / Preheat the oven to 200°C [400°F/Gas mark 6]. When all the pastry shapes have risen (and they will finish rising at different times), spoon the cooled crème pat onto the middle of the pinwheel Danishes and top with a raspberry. Brush the pastries with egg wash and bake for 15–20 minutes, but as soon as the sheets go into the oven, immediately turn the oven temperature down to 180°C [350°F/Gas mark 4]. You will have 2 sheets to bake, but you can bake one sheet at a time. Once golden brown and baked, brush with the glaze while still warm and transfer to a wire rack to cool.

MAKING DECORATIONS AND ASSEMBLY

16 / Temper the white chocolate (page 92), then pour the chocolate over a piece of baking paper. Spread with an offset spatula to smooth a little, then working fast, mix a quarter of the white chocolate with the pink food dye and smooth this over the white chocolate using the offset spatula to create a swirly multicoloured effect. Smooth until thin (about 3mm [⅛in] thick) but not too thin. When the chocolate has semi-set, cut long chocolate shards that will form the 'skirt' later. Set these aside.

17 / Roll out the marzipan on a work surface lightly dusted with icing sugar and cut out shapes for the face and the upper torso/top (a round shape for the face – use a round cutter; and a triangular shape for the upper torso). Colour the Royal Icing with your chosen gel food dye and use to pipe the details onto the marzipan shape for the torso/upper part of the dress.

18 / When the pastries are cool, arrange them on a serving board, so that the 'head' (pecan spiral and braids) is at the top and the 'body' is placed directly below with the pinwheels at the bottom. Apply an extra coating of glaze and stick on the marzipan face and the marzipan top. Arrange the chocolate shards so that they fan out and look like a skirt. Arrange raspberries, edible flowers, sprinkles and any leftover chocolate shards to create the 'hair'.

19 / Use edible paint to paint the facial features onto the circular piece of marzipan and use the pink lustre dust for the cheeks. Pipe a small amount of royal icing onto the eyes and add additional decorations to decorate further!

Valentine's Day

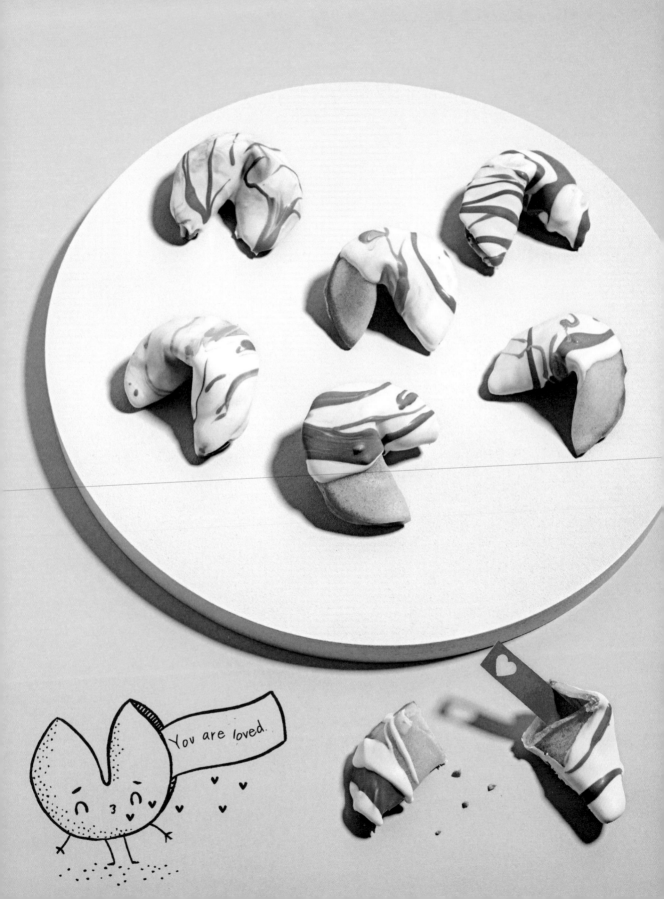

You are loved.

'Oil-painted' Valentine Fortune Cookies

These fortune cookies are a lot easier than they look and sound, and you will quickly get a feel for how to long to bake them, and how to shape them. It's just about making sure they are cooked enough so that they will be crisp and delicious when cooled, but not overcooked, as then they will crack when shaping. You need to work fast while they're hot! Of course, the bonus to making them yourself is that you get to write your own custom Valentine messages! Then you get to pretend you're Jackson Pollock for a while by creating abstract designs on them using coloured chocolate!

MAKES: AROUND 15

3 medium egg whites or aquafaba (about 100ml [⅓ cup plus 2 Tbsp])
80g [½ cup minus 4 tsp] caster or granulated sugar
¼ tsp almond extract
55ml [¼ cup minus 1 tsp] vegetable oil

2 Tbsp water
80g [⅔ cup minus 1 Tbsp] plain [all-purpose] flour
2 Tbsp cornflour [cornstarch]

PLUS
slips of paper

about 200g [7oz] white chocolate (or use candy melts/compound chocolate)
cocoa butter or oil-based food dyes (not water based, otherwise the chocolate will seize!)

Can be made vegan!

1 / Preheat the oven to 180°C [350°F/Gas mark 4]. Line a baking sheet with baking paper or preferably a silicone mat. Write your fortunes onto slips of paper.

2 / Add the egg whites (or aquafaba) and sugar to a large bowl and whisk until frothy. Add the almond extract, oil and water (don't add water if making vegan cookies) and whisk again until just combined. Sift in the flours and whisk to a smooth paste.

3 / Add 1–1½ tsp of the mix onto the lined baking sheet and use the back of the spoon to spread the mix into a thin, 8–9-cm [3¼–3½-in] diameter circle. Repeat to create 2–3 circles (bake a small number at a time because they need to be shaped while they're hot) and bake for 7–8 minutes, or 12–13 minutes if vegan. Keep a close eye and take out of the oven when the edges have just browned (a matter of seconds can make a big difference!).

4 / Once baked, use a spatula or knife to peel the disc off the paper or mat and flip it over. Carefully fold it in half (it helps to wear gloves as they are very hot), then use the edge of a cup to help guide you in pulling the 2 corners down over the sides to meet, to form the classic fortune cookie shape. Slip in the fortune paper. Place in a muffin tin or similar to help the fortune cookie hold its shape while cooling.

5 / Repeat the previous 2 steps until you have used up all the batter.

6 / Melt your white chocolate (or candy melts) in 10–15-second bursts in the microwave, stirring well in between. Colour the chocolate using cocoa butter or oil-based food dye, then dip the fortune cookies into different colours. Drizzle over different colours to create different effects – just have fun with it!

Berry Delicious Valentine's Trifle

What could be more romantic than a giant sharing-sized trifle? With cute cookie people, whipped cream, strawberries, raspberries, crème pâtissière, Swiss roll, cranberry and elderflower jelly... and so big that you probably couldn't finish it in one night, you will have some for leftovers for the next few nights!

SERVES: 10 (IF YOU'RE MAKING A SMALLER TRIFLE OR INDIVIDUAL TRIFLES YOU WILL NEED TO REDUCE THESE QUANTITIES!)

CAKE LAYER
butter, for greasing
4 medium eggs
125g [⅔ cup minus 2 tsp] caster or granulated sugar
125g [1 cup minus 1 Tbsp] self-raising [self-rising] flour (or use gluten-free flour plus ½ tsp xanthan gum and ¾ tsp baking powder)
4 Tbsp raspberry jam

VALENTINE'S COOKIE PEOPLE
½ quantity of Thanksgiving:
Turkeys cookie dough (page 141)
red food dye

FRUIT JELLY LAYER
(Or you can use a store-bought jelly packet and prepare according to the pack instructions)
600ml [2½ cups] cranberry juice (or similar red berry juice)
80g [½ cup minus 4 tsp] caster or granulated sugar
4 Tbsp elderflower syrup
1¼ tsp agar agar powder
OR 4 tsp vege-gel
100g [¾ cup plus 1 tsp] raspberries

CRÈME PÂTISSIÈRE LAYER
900ml [3¾ cups] milk
150g [¾ cup] caster or granulated sugar
50g [½ cup] cornflour [cornstarch]
4 Tbsp vanilla bean paste
9 medium egg yolks

CREAM LAYER
700ml [3 cups] double [heavy] cream

PLUS
130ml [½ cup plus 2 tsp] sherry (or substitute with orange juice or other fruit juice to make non-alcoholic)
3 Tbsp elderflower syrup
200g [1⅔ cups] extra raspberries
275g [2¾ cups] strawberries
about 7 maraschino cherries
sprinkles

1 / First, make the Swiss roll. Preheat the oven to 180°C [350°F/Gas mark 4]. Grease a rectangular [15 x 10-in] Swiss roll tin [jelly roll pan] with butter and line the base with baking paper.

2 / In a large bowl, whisk the eggs and caster sugar together on high speed for 7 minutes. Sift in the self-raising flour in 3 batches, then carefully fold in to avoid deflating the batter too much.

3 / Pour the batter into the prepared tin and bake for 10 minutes until spongy on top.

4 / Once baked, place a chopping board (or similar) on top of the cake and flip so that the chopping board is on the bottom. Remove the baking tin and the baking paper and immediately flip onto a damp tea towel [dish towel]. Trim all the edges, then starting from the longer side, roll up along with the tea towel. Leave the cake to cool fully while wrapped in the tea towel.

5 / Meanwhile, for the Valentine's cookie people, take the Thanksgiving Turkey cookie dough, roll it out and cut into shapes with a person-shaped cutter. Place on a lined baking sheet, then add red food

dye to the remaining dough, reroll and cut out small heart shapes. Place the heart shapes on the people (use a tiny amount of water to help stick), then fold the arms so they're holding the hearts. Use a cocktail stick [toothpick] or modelling tool to press a smile and eyes on each person. Chill in the fridge for 15–30 minutes. At this point preheat the oven to 160°C [325°F/Gas mark 3]. Bake the people for 12 minutes, then transfer to a wire rack and leave to cool. You can customize these people to match you and your loved ones! Try rainbow hearts, piping names on the hearts, adding hair, a hat, sentimental jewellery, etc.

6 / When the Swiss roll is completely cooled, carefully unroll it and spread the jam all over. Roll it up again and slice into 2-cm [¾-in] pieces so that the swirl is visible.

7 / Whisk the sherry (or fruit juice) and elderflower syrup together in a bowl. Lay the Swiss roll slices on a sheet of baking paper and spoon or brush over the mixture.

8 / Next, make the jelly. Add the cranberry juice, caster sugar and elderflower syrup to a pan. Sprinkle over the agar agar powder (or vege-gel) and whisk immediately to combine (don't wait, otherwise the powder can clump together). Place over a high heat and whisk intermittently, until the mixture comes to a boil.

9 / Meanwhile, get a big trifle dish ready. It needs to have a capacity of about 3.6 litres [3.1 quarts] or be around 22cm [8½in] in diameter and 22cm [8½in] deep. Pour the jelly into the trifle dish and immediately add the raspberries so that they are well distributed in the jelly. The agar agar (or vege-gel) both set at room temperature, so don't wait for the mixture to set in the pan! You can leave the trifle dish out at room temperature to set or place in the fridge to set quicker.

10 / Once set, arrange the Swiss roll slices on top of the jelly and all around the circumference of the bowl, so that the swirl can be seen from the outside. Fill the centre with the remaining cake and the extra raspberries.

11 / Next, make the crème pâtissière. Add the milk to a small pan and heat over a medium heat until it comes to a simmer.

12 / While the milk is heating, place the caster sugar, cornflour, vanilla and egg yolks in a bowl and whisk together until thick and smooth.

13 / When the milk just begins to bubble, pour it slowly into the egg mixture, whisking quickly and constantly the whole time (to temper the egg mix and ensure the eggs do not scramble!). Once all the milk is combined, pour the whole mixture back into the pan and continue heating over a medium-high heat. Allow the mixture to bubble while whisking constantly as it thickens. If it starts looking lumpy at any point, just temporarily remove from the heat and keep whisking as fast as you can.

14 / Once the crème pat is thickened and holds a trail when the whisk is removed from the mixture, remove from the heat and transfer a third to a piping [pastry] bag and cut a tip. Pipe a border above the cake layer so that it shows from the outside of the glass. Spoon in more crème pat to fill the centre.

15 / Cut the top off the strawberries and slice in half, then arrange around the circumference (similar to the Swiss roll), with the cut strawberry side facing outwards and pressed against the glass. Pipe or spoon any remaining custard in the centre.

16 / Leave the custard to cool, then whip the cream to soft peaks and transfer ⅕ to a piping bag. Cut a medium opening, and pipe this in all the gaps between the strawberries. Pipe any remaining cream into the middle, then spoon the rest of the cream on top and piled high. Decorate with the maraschino cherries and the Valentine's cookie people, then scatter sprinkles over the whipped cream to finish.

"Wipe away those trifling matters (or better yet, eat them)."

Robot Fondant Fancies

Fondant fancies are one of my favourite miniature treats, so I fancied making them into robots. These can be a little fiddly to decorate, but take your time and make sure the cake and buttercream are chilled at the right points. Adding all the decorations also helps to disguise any imperfections! Make sure you add hearts and personalized valentine's messages to their little robot screens too. Feel free to make these all slightly different sizes, just to create a bit of fun and personality.

```
Can be made vegan!
```

MAKES: 25

VEGAN CAKE
vegan butter, for greasing
1¾ tsp white wine vinegar
390ml [1½ cups plus 2 Tbsp] soy milk
155ml [⅔ cup minus 1 tsp] sunflower oil or other neutral-tasting oil
1 Tbsp vanilla bean paste
grated zest of 1 lemon
¼ tsp salt
350g [2⅔ cups] self-raising [self-rising] flour
260g [1⅓ cups] caster or granulated sugar
1¼ Tbsp baking powder

DAIRY-BASED CAKE
225g [1 cup] butter, softened at room temperature, plus extra for greasing
225g [1¾ cups] self-raising [self-rising] flour
225g [1 cup plus 2 Tbsp] caster or granulated sugar
4 medium eggs
1 Tbsp vanilla bean paste
grated zest of 2 lemons

MARZIPAN (OR USE STOREBOUGHT)
100g [¾ cup minus ½ Tbsp] icing [confectioners'] sugar, plus extra for dusting
100g [1 cup] finely ground almonds
35g [1¼oz] egg white (or aquafaba)
¼ tsp almond extract

BUTTERCREAM
150g [⅔ cup] butter (or vegan butter, use one that is at least 75% fat content)
220g [1½ cups] icing [confectioners'] sugar
1 tsp vanilla bean paste
1–2 Tbsp milk (omit this if making vegan)

FONDANT ICING
500g [17oz] white fondant
75–100ml [5–7 Tbsp] water
pink, green and yellow gel food dyes

PLUS
4–6 Tbsp strawberry jam
sprinkles, fondant and extra food dye to decorate

1 – for the vegan cake / Use vegan butter to grease a 22-cm [8½-in] square tin, then line with baking paper. Preheat the oven to 170°C [340°F/Gas mark 3].

2 – for the vegan cake / In a large bowl, mix the vinegar with the soy milk until it curdles and thickens. Add the rest of the wet ingredients, including the grated lemon zest and salt and stir together. In a separate large bowl, combine all the dry ingredients together. Add the dry ingredients to the wet and whisk until just combined. Pour the batter immediately into the prepared tin and bake for 30–40 minutes until a skewer or knife inserted into the centre of the cake comes out clean. Leave to cool in the tin for 10 minutes, then run a knife around the edge of the tin and turn out onto a wire rack. Peel off the baking paper, and leave to cool completely.

1 – for the dairy-based cake / Use butter to grease a 22-cm [8½-in] square tin, then line with baking paper. Preheat the oven to 150°C [300°F/Gas mark 2].

2 – for the dairy-based cake / Add all the ingredients to a bowl and beat until smooth and combined. Use a spatula to scrape the batter into the prepared tin and bake for about 40 minutes, or until a skewer or knife inserted into the centre of the cake comes out clean. Leave to cool in the tin for 10 minutes, then run a knife around the edge of the tin and turn out onto a wire rack. Peel off the baking paper, and leave to cool completely.

3 / While the cake cools, make the marzipan. Combine all the ingredients in a bowl and stir until it all comes together into a smooth ball. Wrap in plastic wrap ready for later.

4 / Next, make the buttercream. Add the butter and icing sugar to a bowl, then cream together using an electric whisk (or in a stand mixer fitted with the ballloon whisk attachment) until light and fluffy. Add the vanilla and whisk again for a few seconds. Add the milk (if you are not making vegan buttercream) and stir in until it is a spreadable consistency. Cover with plastic wrap and set aside for now.

5 / When the cake is cool, wrap in plastic wrap and chill in the freezer for 1–2 hours (this will make it easier to cut neatly later!).

6 / When the cake is chilled and firm, spread jam over the top, then roll out the marzipan thinly on a work surface lightly dusted with icing sugar and place on top of the jam layer. Cut into 25 pieces, trimming the edges if necessary to neaten.

7 / Use a palette knife to spread buttercream thinly over the 4 exposed sides of each fondant fancy.

8 / Place the remaining buttercream in a piping [pastry] bag and cut a medium tip. Pipe a small amount of buttercream into the centre on top of each fondant fancy. Dip your fingertip in water and use to press down the peaks of each mound of buttercream. Chill the fondant fancies in the fridge until the buttercream is firm to touch.

9 / Next, make the fondant icing. Tear the fondant into chunks and add to a stand mixer fitted with the paddle attachment. Mix on low speed until the fondant is smooth. Start gradually adding the water while continuing to mix until the fondant is smooth and a pourable consistency. A stand mixer is ideal, although you can also do this using a handheld electric whisk. Divide the fondant icing between 3 bowls and stir through gel food colouring until the desired colour is achieved.

10 / Pierce the base of a fondant fancy with a fork (at an angle to make it easier to slide off again), then hold over a bowl while you spoon the icing over the top, making sure to cover all the sides. Remove the excess drips, then slide off the fork and onto a wire rack. Repeat until all the fancies are covered in different colours. Leave for a few hours until set.

11 / Lift the fondant fancies from the wire rack and place in mini cupcake cases which have been folded into squares. Decorate as robots using various sprinkles (attach using some of the fondant icing) and add painted fondant for the screens. You can decorate your robots however you like! Paint hearts on their screens and your loved one's initals for a personal touch.

- VALENTINE'S DAY -

"To work to your full potential, you need to rest and recharge your batteries."

Valentine's Cherry Millefeuille

Millefeuille can sound intimidating because it is puff pastry and looks so delicately and neatly stacked. However, the rough puff pastry used here is a lot quicker and easier to make than full puff pastry – and if you want to make things even quicker then you can use store-bought puff pastry. Even if yours isn't picture perfect, your Valentine will appreciate the effort you've gone to (hopefully), especially if you top it with the glitter cherries!

MAKES: 8 INDIVIDUAL PORTIONS

ROUGH PUFF PASTRY
(you can use storebought puff pastry if you like!)
70g [⅓ cup minus 1 tsp] frozen butter (leave in freezer for at least 5 hours)
350g [2⅔ cups] plain [all-purpose] flour, plus extra for dusting
1 tsp salt
135–150ml [9–10 Tbsp] cold water (as cold as possible)
200g [¾ cup plus 2 Tbsp] frozen butter, divided into 2 portions (leave in freezer for at least 5 hours), grated

4 tsp caster or granulated sugar, to sprinkle

CRÈME DIPLOMATE FILLING
500ml [2 cups plus 2 Tbsp] milk
150g [¾ cup] caster or granulated sugar
60g [⅔ cup] cornflour [cornstarch]
1½ Tbsp vanilla bean paste
7 egg yolks
30g [2 Tbsp] butter
3 tsp freeze-dried cherry powder
finely grated zest of 1 lemon

130ml [½ cup plus 2 tsp] double [heavy] cream
pink gel food dye

ICING GLAZE
300g [2 cups plus 2 Tbsp] icing [confectioners'] sugar, plus extra
about 50ml [3½ Tbsp] milk
red gel food dye

PLUS
16 cherries
edible glitter
500g [4 cups] fresh raspberries
black gel food dye

1 / First, make the rough puff pastry. Grate the 70g [⅓ cup minus 1 tsp] frozen butter into the flour and salt. Stir, then add enough cold water to combine into a ball.

Tip: For best results, work in a cold room and on a cold work surface. You shouldn't need to chill the dough between rolling out and book folds, but if it's a hot day or a warm room, you may notice the butter starting to melt through the layers, so you will just

need to just wrap the dough in plastic wrap and chill in the fridge for 30–60 minutes.

2 / Roll out the dough on a lightly floured work surface to a 18 x 40-cm [7 x 16-in] rectangle, with the longest side facing you. Scatter 100g [7 Tbsp] of the grated frozen butter into the middle two-thirds of the rectangle, then do a book fold: fold each side to the middle so that they meet, then fold together like closing a book. Rotate 90 degrees, roll out to the

same size again and repeat the book fold with the second 100g [7 Tbsp] of frozen grated butter. Rotate again, roll out and do one last book fold (no butter this time). Chill in the fridge for at least 2 hours, or preferably overnight before using.

3 / Meanwhile, make the crème diplomate. Add the milk to a small pan and heat over a medium heat until it comes to a simmer.

4 / While the milk is heating, place the caster sugar, cornflour, vanilla bean paste and egg yolks in a bowl and whisk until thick and smooth.

5 / When the milk just begins to bubble, pour it slowly into the egg mixture, whisking quickly and constantly the whole time (to temper the egg mix and ensure the eggs do not scramble!). Once all the milk is combined, pour the mixture back into the pan and continue heating over a medium-high heat. Allow the crème pâtissière to bubble while whisking constantly as it thickens. If the custard starts looking lumpy at any point, just temporarily remove from the heat and keep whisking as fast as you can.

6 / Once the crème pat is thickened and holds a thick trail when the whisk is lifted from the pan (it should be very, very thick, as it will be lightened with whipped cream later – make sure you keep whisking and heating until it has become as thick as it can get!), remove from the heat and stir through the butter until it is melted and combined. Place in a bowl and cover with plastic wrap (ensuring it touches the surface of the crème pat to prevent it forming a skin). Place in the fridge for about 2 hours until chilled.

7 / When the pastry is chilled, preheat the oven to 200°C [400°F/Gas mark 6] and line a large flat (no vertical sides) baking sheet with baking paper. Divide the pastry into 2 pieces. Roll out the first piece on a lightly floured surface to about 25 x 35cm [10 x 14in]. Place on the lined baking sheet, sprinkle with a teaspoon of sugar, then cover with another sheet of baking paper and a second baking sheet (this is to prevent the pastry rising too high!). Bake for 15 minutes.

8 / Carefully flip the pastry/sheets over, remove the top baking sheet and paper and sprinkle with another teaspoon of sugar. Replace the baking paper and sheet on top and bake for a further 10 minutes, or until flaky and golden throughout. Transfer to a wire rack and leave to cool.

9 / Repeat this baking process with the second half of the pastry set aside earlier. (You could in theory bake both at once with a good convection oven, although this requires 4 large, flat baking sheets, which most of us don't have!)

10 / When the pastry is cool, place on a chopping board (it should be rigid, not floppy, if properly baked, so will be easy to move) and trim the edges so that they are straight. Cut out 12 x 5 x 10-cm [2 x 4-in] rectangles using a sharp knife and repeat with the second pastry sheet. You should have 24 rectangles.

Tip: Alternatively, you can cut the pastry to size before baking. You may have to bake this in 3 batches, and optionally use a sharp knife to get a neat edge after baking. But there's less mess with flaky pastry going everywhere from cutting it. Both ways work – just do whichever way round you prefer!

11 / For the icing glaze, place the icing sugar in a bowl and while whisking, gradually add the milk (you may not need it all) until it is a spreadable consistency, but not so runny that it will run off the pastry, and not so thick that it won't spread. Test this on a spare piece of pastry if you're not sure!

12 / Transfer a fifth of the icing to a separate bowl, add red food dye to colour and transfer to a piping [pastry] bag. Cut a small tip.

13 / Transfer the remaining white icing to another piping bag and cut a small tip. Working quickly to avoid the icing drying out before marbling it, pipe the white icing in a border around a pastry rectangle, then pipe more white icing to fill. Pipe red dots in rows on top of the white icing, then drag a cocktail stick [toothpick] through to create little heart shapes. Repeat for a total of 8 glazed pastry rectangles. Leave to set.

14 / While the icing is setting, make the cherry decoration toppers. Cut the bottoms of cherries so they sit flush. Wet the cherries with a little water, then apply a compact layer of glitter using a paintbrush (the water will make it stick) and set aside for now.

15 / Remove the chilled crème pat from the fridge; it will be lumpy and stiff, so just whisk it to make it smooth once again. Add the freeze-dried cherry powder and lemon zest and whisk to combine again. To make it into a lighter crème diplomate, whipped cream needs to folded through. Whip the cream to soft peaks, then fold this through the crème pat in 3 stages until there are no visible streaks of cream remaining. Stir in pink food dye to colour, then transfer to a piping bag and cut a medium tip.

16 / Place 1 plain pastry rectangle on a serving plate. Pipe the crème diplomate in blobs on top, alternating with raspberries to make a pattern. Place a second plain pastry rectangle on top and repeat the filling. Place the glazed pastry rectangle on top, then top with a pair of glitter cherries. Repeat to make 8 millefeuilles.

17 / To finish off decorating, thicken the white glaze by stirring through a little extra icing sugar until it is more pipeable and thick, then dye a small amount black. Place the white and black icing into separate piping bags and cut a very small tip. Secure the cherry stems together with a dot of white icing and pipe on the eyes and mouth using the white and black icing. Best served as soon as possible after assembling!

"Practice makes you a cherry good baker."

- VALENTINE'S DAY -

Cursed Apple Cake

This cake is the perfect cursed centrepiece for your Halloween celebrations! All the decorative elements on their own are not difficult, but when you put them together, it looks really striking. Guests love it when they realize that the red drips are actually a very tasty salted caramel. Set the remaining caramel aside in a bowl for sure, as extra is always appreciated!

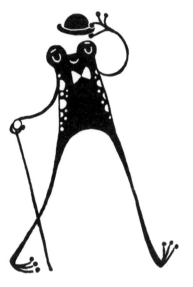

"Don't froget to tell yourself: 'I am toadally ribbiting!'"

SERVES: 20–30 (DEPENDING ON WHICH CAKE YOU CHOOSE TO MAKE)

CANDIED APPLE
(this makes more caramel than you need, but it's hard to dip the apple if you make less. Feel free to make extra candied apples for snacking alongside the cake.)
1 twig, cleaned
1 red apple
70ml [⅓ cup minus 2 tsp] water
350g [1¾ cups] caster or granulated sugar
50g [¼ cup] liquid glucose or light corn syrup (you can replace this with sugar, although this increases the likelihood of the sugar crystallizing, especially if you're repeatedly dipping several apples into it)
red gel food dye

RED SALTED CARAMEL DRIP
90ml [6 Tbsp] water
240g [1¼ cups minus 2 tsp] caster or granulated sugar
225ml [1 cup minus 1 Tbsp] double [heavy] cream (or coconut milk to make vegan – you won't taste the coconut flavour due to the strong flavours of the cake)
fine table salt, to taste
red gel food dye

FONDANT FROGS
100g [3½oz] green fondant
4 edible eyes

PLUS
choose a cake recipe (pages 10–26), baked and cooled
1 quantity of American Buttercream (page 31) or Italian Meringue Buttercream (page 32) (I recommend that you add a little white food dye to your buttercream to get more of a pure white colour)
white food dye for buttercream

Can be made vegan!

1 / First, make the candied apple. Poke the twig into the top of the apple so that it is secure. Add the water, sugar and liquid glucose to a small pan and heat over a high heat until it reaches hard crack, which is 150°C [302°F] on a sugar thermometer. If you don't have one, you can test if it's done by dropping a small amount of candy into cold water; it's ready if it hardens straightaway. If it's still soft, boil for longer.

Tip: Avoid stirring the candy at all – your sugar won't burn as long as you don't make the temperature too high. You can swirl the pan a tiny bit, but you should barely need to do this. If you stir, the sugar is likely to crystallize and the mixture will get thick and grainy.

2 / When ready, add red gel food dye until it's a deep red colour and swirl very gently to combine – it will spread very easily, so don't stir! Dip the apple in, tipping the pan a little to help cover the whole surface. Allow any excess to drip off, then place on a piece of baking paper and leave for 15 minutes, or until completely set.

3 / Next, make the red salted caramel drip. Heat the water and sugar in a saucepan over a low-medium heat, stirring occasionally, until the sugar has completely dissolved. Then turn up the heat and wait (don't stir) until the sugar turns an amber colour. You can swirl the pan around to even out the colour.

4 / When the sugar syrup has turned a deep amber colour, remove the pan from the heat, add the cream in one go and stir constantly with a balloon whisk. The caramel will bubble up so be careful at this stage! Return the pan to a low heat and continue stirring until all the sugar has dissolved and you have a smooth, creamy sauce. Mix in enough red food dye to get a vibrant red. Pour the sauce into a medium bowl and sprinkle with a little salt to taste. Don't add too much; it's better to add too little than too much. Leave the caramel to cool in the fridge for about 2 hours, or until thick.

Tip: Before using the caramel drip, you can test the consistency of the caramel drip on a glass, or on the back of the cake. Wait a few minutes to see how far the drip travels before working on the whole cake. You need to ensure that the caramel is the optimum temperature so that it doesn't just drip off the cake (too warm) or not drip enough (too cold/stiff). If it's too thick, microwave it in 2-second bursts.

5 / To make the fondant frogs, make a round blob of green fondant for the body, then squish it down slightly. Add another round blob on top for the head,

then use a knife to cut halfway through this to create the open mouth. Attach small thin circles on top for the eyes, then press edible eyes on. Shape a long tapered piece of fondant for the legs, then fold it so that the tapered ends meet. Place this on one side of the frog, then repeat for the other side. Add small round thin circles for the feet, pressing to make them stick to the underside of the frog, then use a knife to cut slits to represent webbed feet.

6 / Make sure the cakes are cool before assembling. Stack and crumb-coat the cakes (see pages 27–28). Spread another layer of buttercream all over the chilled crumb coat using a palette knife and smooth again. Chill in the fridge until firm.

7 / When the cake is firm, place the chilled red caramel into a piping [pastry] bag and cut a small tip. Pipe controlled drips down the side of the cake, varying the lengths. Use a palette knife to smooth red caramel over the top of the cake, then add the candied apple. Position a frog at the end of a drip, as if the drip is going into its mouth. Add extra caramel to its mouth and dripping around. Position a second frog peeking out from behind the apple.

STEP 7 ▼

Key Slime Pie Cauldron

A fun spooky variation of the classic key lime pie, but don't be fooled by the monsters spewing out on top, this bake is one that you will want to make and eat time and time again. There are so many variations you can create with this too, using different types of meringue monsters! Come up with your own version and show off your witchy baking skills!

SERVES: 6–8 (MAKES: 1 X 22-CM [8½-IN] TART)

CRUST
220g [7¾oz] Oreos (these are vegan but not gluten free, although you can buy gluten-free versions to make this recipe gluten free)
80g [⅓ cup] butter, melted (or use vegan butter, at least 75–80% fat content)

DAIRY-BASED FILLING
3 medium egg yolks (you will use the leftover egg whites for the meringue monsters in the topping!)
400g [1¾ cups] condensed milk
finely grated zest and juice of 4 limes (about 100ml [½ cup minus 1 Tbsp] juice)

VEGAN FILLING
250g [1 cup plus 2 Tbsp] vegan condensed milk
40g [½ cup minus 2 tsp] cornflour [cornstarch]
200ml [¾ cup plus 2 Tbsp] coconut milk
finely grated zest and juice of 4 limes (about 100ml [½ cup minus 1 Tbsp] juice)

20g [1½ Tbsp] caster or granulated sugar

TOPPING
200ml [¾ cup plus 2 Tbsp] double [heavy] cream (or use a whippable oat milk to make vegan)
20g [2¼ Tbsp] icing [confectioners'] sugar
green food dye

MERINGUE MONSTERS
see page 76, making them green and white, in various shapes, with edible eyes

> "Ssssstop and unwind from time to time."

> Can be made vegan!

1 / First, for the crust, crush the cookies in a food processor or place in a bag and bash with a rolling pin. Transfer to a bowl and stir through the melted butter (or vegan butter). Press the cookie mixture into the base and up the sides of a 22-cm [8½-in] tart tin and chill in the freezer for 10 minutes.

2 / Meanwhile, preheat the oven to 170°C [340°F/ Gas mark 3]. Bake the crust for 10 minutes, then leave to cool completely (if making vegan, don't bake, just pop into the fridge or freezer to chill until firm). Leave the oven on.

3 – for the dairy-based filling / Whisk the egg yolks until broken up. Add the condensed milk and whisk until smooth and combined. Whisk in the lime zest and juice, then pour onto the cooled crust and bake for about 15 minutes. Leave to cool, then refrigerate for at least 6 hours, or overnight.

3 – for the vegan filling / Whisk the condensed milk and cornflour together in a pan off the heat (whisk immediately to stop the cornflour clumping!). Add the coconut milk (it's fine if it's in lumps, it will melt on the heat), lime zest, lime juice and sugar and stir over a medium heat, allowing it to boil a little and whisking constantly to thicken without lumps. If it starts getting lumpy, just take the pan off the heat for a moment and continue whisking vigorously, then return to the heat. The mixture should be thick and firmly holds a trail when the whisk is lifted out of the mixture. Pour over the cookie base. Cover with plastic wrap and leave to cool, then refrigerate for 6 hours, or overnight.

4 / For the topping, whip the cream (or whippable oat milk), icing sugar and a little green food dye to colour together in a stand mixer (or use a handheld electric whisk) fitted with the balloon whisk attachment on low speed to start, then increasing the speed to high. When the cream reaches soft peaks, put a small amount into a piping [pastry] bag (don't add too much at a time as the cream at the top will become overwhipped due to all the piping action) and cut a tip. Pipe over the chilled base in lots of different sizes.

5 / Add some meringue monsters in some gaps, then pipe more cream to fill the gaps and to create height. Keep adding more meringue monsters as you work.

Make similar monsters to the ones pictured, or create your own scene! Maybe the cauldron could be spawning frogs instead? Or dribbling 'blood'?

STEP 4 ▼

- HALLOWEEN -

"Sometimes there are storms: try to roll with it instead of spinning down."

Hurricane Spider Swiss Roll

This 'hurricane'-style Swiss roll (named as such because of the pattern created by the 2 colours swirled together) is made using a chiffon cake technique, so it is soft like a pillow. This, plus the addition of the cream and jam filling makes you want to have slice after slice after slice, as well as some gooey chocolate brownies to finish! To make sure the hurricane pattern comes out nicely and the cake rolls without a big crack, make sure to read and reread the recipe first before you start.

SERVES: 8–10

CAKE: FOR THE COLOUR
1 Tbsp unsweetened cocoa powder (or 1 Tbsp charcoal powder)
2 Tbsp hot water
black gel food dye

CAKE: EGG YOLK MIXTURE
butter, for greasing
5 medium egg yolks
35g [2½ Tbsp] caster or granulated sugar

pinch of salt
60ml [¼ cup] vegetable oil
60ml [¼ cup] whole milk
100g [¾ cup] plain [all-purpose] flour (or use a gluten-free flour blend and ¼ tsp xanthan gum)
2 tsp cornflour [cornstarch]

CAKE: EGG WHITE MIXTURE
5 medium egg whites

65g [⅓ cup plus 1 tsp] caster or granulated sugar

FILLING
4 Tbsp strawberry or raspberry jam
140ml [⅔ cup minus 4 tsp] double [heavy] cream
30g [3½ Tbsp] icing [confectioners'] sugar
red gel food dye
1 Tbsp vanilla bean paste

MARSHMALLOW WEB
6 medium white marshmallows

BROWNIE SPIDERS
1 quantity of Brownie Spiders (page 81), alternatively if short on time you can use Oreo cookies or similar

1 / Preheat the oven to 160°C [325°F/Gas mark 3]. Grease the base and sides of a 27 x 35-cm [10¾ x 14-in] Swiss roll tin [jelly roll pan] or baking sheet with shallow sides with butter and line with baking paper, covering the base and the 2 longer sides.

2 / First, for the cake colour, stir the 1 Tbsp cocoa powder (or charcoal powder) and 2 Tbsp hot (but not boiling) water together in a bowl. Set aside for now.

3 / Add all the 'cake: egg yolk mixture' ingredients to a large bowl and whisk until smooth.

4 / In a separate bowl, make the 'cake: egg white mixture'. Use a handheld electric whisk or stand mixer fitted with the balloon whisk attachment and whisk the egg whites on medium speed until foamy. Add the caster sugar and continue whisking until soft

peaks form. For this cake, you want the peaks to flop over slightly at the tips, rather than point upwards. If you whisk beyond this point, you may get cracks in your finished cake when rolling.

5 / Fold the egg whites into the egg yolk mixture, adding a third at a time. Your batter should be of pourable consistency in order to avoid cracks later. Pour 200g [7oz] into another bowl and stir in the cocoa powder (or black charcoal) mixture until combined. Add enough black food to colour a deep black colour.

6 / Pour the white batter into the prepared tin, and spread out evenly. Pour the black batter on top and spread out with a spatula. Use a chopstick or the handle of a butter knife to swirl the batter, dragging the chopstick or spoon left and right along the longest side, then repeating the same motion along the shortest side. Bang the sheet once to release any large air bubbles.

7 / Bake for 20 minutes, or until a knife or skewer inserted into the centre of the cake comes out clean and the top is spongy and springs back. Using the sides of the baking paper, lift the cake onto a wire rack and leave to cool.

8 / When the cake is cool, place a sheet of baking paper on top, then a chopping board or similar flat board and flip the whole cake over. Peel off the baking paper, then trim all the edges (they are drier, so leaving them could cause the cake to crack). On one of the shorter ends, cut 5 shallow slits into the cake, then spread over the jam. Add the cream, icing sugar, red food dye and vanilla to a bowl and whip to soft peaks. Spread on top of the jam, then roll up from one of the shorter sides using the baking paper to help you. Leave loosely covered with the baking paper and chill in the fridge for a few minutes.

9 / Place the Swiss roll on a serving tray and trim the ends so that the spiral shows clearly.

10 / Place the marshmallows in a bowl and heat in the microwave on high for 15 seconds. The marshmallow should stretch and become web-like when stretched. Dip your thumb and index finger into the marshamallow and move your fingers to get the marshmallow to stretch and look stringy. When it looks nice and stringy, stretch it over the cake, forming webs. Don't move the web once it's in place, as it will take the top layer of cake with it! If this happens, you can easily cover it with a spider. This marshmallow technique might feel unfamiliar at first, but you will quickly get the hang of it.

11 / Decorate with the Brownie Spiders to finish!

STEP 6 ▼

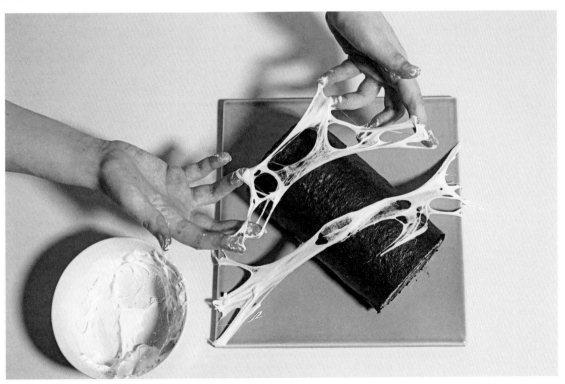

Meringue Monsters

These are just some of the shapes you could make, but once you get started, your own creativity will take over and you'll make all sorts of monster shapes! These are so freeing and fun to create. It's very difficult to actually go wrong. Serve them on their own, or on the Key Slime Pie (page 69) or any other cake (pages 10–26).

Can be made vegan!

MAKES: 2 LARGE SHEETS OF HALLOWEEN MERINGUES, OR 3 MEDIUM SHEETS

MERINGUE

3 medium egg
   whites/120g [4oz] (to
   make vegan, use
   aquafaba/canned
   chickpea water)
pinch of cream of tartar
   (optional)
210g [1 cup plus 2 tsp]
   caster or granulated
   sugar

PLUS

gel food dyes
edible glue (or similar,
   or just mix a little icing
   [confectioners'] sugar
   and water to a paste)
edible eyes

Note: The method for the vegan meringues is essentially the same, it just takes a little longer to whisk to soft peaks initially. Also, the vegan version is better baked until completely dry in the centre, and they are more prone to getting sticky on the outside when exposed to humidity. You can always put them back in the oven on a low heat, and this will make them dry again.

1 / Preheat the oven to 100°C [212°F/Gas mark ¼]. Add the egg whites (or aquafaba) to a stand mixer fitted with the balloon whisk attachment (you can use an electric whisk but you will be whisking for a long time so a stand mixer is ideal). Mix on high speed until you have soft peaks, then whisk in the cream of tartar, and then gradually add the sugar, 1 Tbsp at a time, whisking for about 30–60 seconds after each addition. It is important to add the sugar very slowly so that it all dissolves properly.

2 / When all the sugar has been incorporated (the meringue should feel smooth, not gritty between your fingers), divide the meringue between different bowls depending on how many colours you want. Stir the gel food dye into each bowl until evenly distributed.

3 / Pipe shapes for different monsters onto baking paper or a silicone mat. See below for a few ideas. Bake for 45–60 minutes for meringues that are gooey in the centre; or 1 hour 30 minutes, then switch off the oven and leave the oven door closed for a few hours for completely crisp and dry meringues.

4 / Use edible glue or icing sugar mixed with water to stick the edible eyes to the meringues.

MERINGUE GHOSTS
Fill a piping bag with meringue, cut a medium tip and pipe meringue kisses. Using your fingers, pinch the sides to create little arms, or pipe on little arms.

TALL GHOSTS WITH A RIPPLED EFFECT
Alternate between squeezing your piping bag and then stopping while working your way upwards.

WORMS
Squeeze more at the beginning so that the head of the worm is bigger, then gradually squeeze less as you move down the tail.

Use a sultane-style piping tip to create meringues with holes in the centre. Once you get the hang of it, play about with other effects! Add red gel food dye for blood (you can thin this with a little water), and black gel food dye for details. Also try making other creatures, such as frogs or pumpkins with edible eyes! See where the meringue takes you.

"Creep calm and carry on."

Pannacotta Eyeballs

You'll feel a bit like a fancy chef making these and splashing coulis artfully around the plate, but they don't merely look arty – the panacotta sets to the perfect creamy consistency with this quantity of setting agent, and contrasts beautifully with the strawberry coulis and small amount of acidity from the lemon juice. These are a perfect light and refreshing dessert after a big Halloween meal.

Note: You can use either vegan Vege-gel, or gelatine to set the panacottas.

MAKES: 12 X 7-CM [2¾-IN] PANACOTTAS (OR YOU CAN MAKE LARGER BUT FEWER)

PANACOTTA
500ml [2 cups plus 2 Tbsp] milk (or use soy milk to make vegan)
2 tsp Vege-gel (about 1 sachet) OR 3½ tsp gelatine powder
500ml [2 cups plus 2 Tbsp] double [heavy] cream (or coconut milk to make vegan)

120g [⅔ cup] caster or granulated sugar
1 Tbsp vanilla bean paste (or 2 vanilla pods [beans], split in half lengthways and seeds scraped out)

STRAWBERRY COULIS
500g [2⅔ cups] frozen strawberries (or use fresh and hull them first)
75–175g [½ cup plus ½ Tbsp–1¼ cups] icing [confectioners'] sugar (or to taste depending on sweetness of fruit)
60ml [¼ cup] water
3 tsp lemon juice

PLUS
1–2 kiwis, peeled and sliced as thinly as possible
black gel food dye

> Can be made vegan!

1 – if using Vege-gel / Add the milk to a small pan, sprinkle over the Vege-gel and whisk immediately to prevent clumping. Add the cream, sugar and vanilla bean paste or seeds and pod and whisk while heating over a medium-high heat until the mixture comes to the boil. Boil for 1 minute, whisking constantly.

1 – if using gelatine / Add the milk to a small pan, sprinkle over the gelatine and leave to soften for 5 minutes. Add the cream, sugar and vanilla seeds and pod and heat over a low heat, stirring frequently. Don't let the milk simmer or boil otherwise this stops the gelatine working (whereas vege-gel is the opposite and needs to boil!). Heat until the gelatine has all dissolved: check by rubbing some milk between your fingers – it should feel smooth if all dissolved, and should dissolve quite quickly. It dissolves at body temperature, so you don't need to heat it much.

2 / Remove and discard the vanilla pod (if using), then pour the mixture into 12 x 7-cm [2¾-in] silicone moulds or 12 glazed or glass small bowls and leave to set in the fridge. The Vege-gel-based one will set quickly (within 3 hours), but gelatine will set slower (at least 4 hours)

3 / For the coulis, if using frozen strawberries, simmer all the ingredients in a pan until the strawberries have thawed. Transfer to a blender and blend until smooth. Push through a sieve before using. If using fresh strawberries, blend with the sugar, water and lemon juice. Place in a pan and simmer for 1 minute, then sieve.

4 / To assemble, spoon 2 generous Tbsp of coulis onto serving plates, allowing for some splashes. Turn the panacotta out and carefully place on top of the coulis. Place a slice of kiwi in the centre of the panacotta. Use some of the reserved sieved fruit to redden the kiwi eye, then use a dot of black food dye to create a pupil. Serve straightaway.

Brownie Spiders

Ordinarily, you probably wouldn't want to be eating spiders, but these BROWNIE spiders change everything. They are extremely decadent with just the right amount of gooeyness – just as a brownie should be.

MAKES: A CLUTTER OF SPIDERS

BROWNIES
220g [1 cup minus 1 tsp] unsalted butter, melted (or use salted butter and omit the added salt), plus extra for greasing
½ tsp salt
3 Tbsp vegetable oil
200g [1 cup] caster or granulated sugar
180g [1 cup minus 1½ Tbsp] dark muscovado [soft brown] sugar

4 large eggs
1 tsp vanilla bean paste
140g [1 cup plus 2 tsp] plain [all-purpose] flour (or use gluten-free flour plus ½ tsp xanthan gum)
100g [1 cup] unsweetened cocoa powder
250g [1½ cups] dark [bittersweet] chocolate (at least 70% cocoa solids), roughly chopped

PLUS
50g [¼ cup] dark [bittersweet] chocolate, broken into pieces
pretzel sticks (or similar) for legs
edible eyes

Oreo biscuits (or similar) can be used instead of brownies to make the spider bodies.

1 / Preheat the oven to 170°C [340°F/Gas mark 3]. Grease a 23-cm [9-in] square tin with butter and line with baking paper, allowing the baking paper to extend up 2 of the sides to make lifting out easier later.

2 / Place the butter, salt, oil and both sugars in a stand mixer fitted with a balloon whisk attachment (or use a handheld electric whisk) and whisk until just combined. Add the eggs and vanilla and whisk on high speed until pale in colour. Sift in the flour and cocoa powder and fold in gently. Add the roughly chopped chocolate and fold in again. Don't overmix after adding the flour!

3 / Pour the batter into the prepared tin and bake for 20–30 minutes until no longer liquid in the middle, but it should still look technically 'undercooked'. It will finish cooking as it cools. Leave to cool in the tin for 5 minutes, then lift out using the baking paper tabs, and place on a wire rack to finish cooling. Once cool, wrap in plastic wrap and freeze for 30 minutes (this makes cutting out the shapes a lot easier and neater).

4 / Use circular cutters to stamp out shapes. You can cut out different sizes for different-sized spiders! Place the leftover brownie cuttings on a plate to be nibbled at, so none is wasted.

5 / Melt the extra 50g [¼ cup] chocolate in a microwaveable bowl in 15–30-second bursts. Break up pretzel sticks and attach to the brownies using the melted chocolate. Use more chocolate for where the pretzels join each other. Ensure your chocolate isn't too warm, as you will be holding the leg in place for a long time before it sticks! Use more melted chocolate to attach the edible eyes.

Tip: You can also make baby spiders by slicing some of the brownie circles thinner, and using smaller pretzel legs.

Christmas Cookies

'Christmas cookies' has a certain ring to it, right? The alliteration of it entices you in, then the cuteness makes you stay for a moment longer and then that first bite makes you want to stay forever! These thick, chunky-style cookies are baked at a higher temperature than normal cookies to ensure that the outside is crisp and the inside is gooey. You can also experiment with adding different types of chocolate and nuts but don't reduce the quantity, as this is what helps make these cookies so thick and chunky. Just make sure not to overbake these, and you will be in Christmas cookie heaven.

MAKES: ABOUT 30 (40G [1½OZ] EACH) OR MAKE HALF THE NUMBER BUT JUMBO SIZE!

115g [½ cup] unsalted butter
½ tsp salt
130g [⅔ cup] soft light brown sugar
85g [½ cup minus 1 Tbsp] caster or granulated sugar
1 tsp vanilla bean paste
2 medium eggs
1½ tsp baking powder

250g [2 cups minus 2 tsp] plain [all-purpose] flour (or use gluten-free flour plus 1 tsp xanthan gum)
1 Tbsp cornflour [cornstarch]
400g [14oz] chocolate, roughly chopped (half white and half dark, or experiment with what chocolate you add! See note about caramelized

white chocolate on page 86)
150g [1 cup plus 1½ Tbsp] walnuts, toasted and roughly chopped (although you can use any nuts you like, or a combination of different nuts)

ROYAL ICING
see page 94

PLUS
add 20g [4 tsp] unsweetened cocoa powder to half the dough to create darker chocolate dough (optional)
food dyes of choice
sweets [candies]
edible eyes

1 / Line 2–3 large baking sheets with baking paper. Place the butter, salt and both sugars in a stand mixer fitted with a balloon whisk attachment (or use a handheld electric whisk) and whisk on high speed until light and fluffy. Add the vanilla and whisk to combine. Add the eggs, one at a time, whisking after each addition until combined. Add the baking powder and both flours and stir by hand until mostly mixed in but some visible flour still remains (this is to avoid overmixing and overworking the gluten).

2 / **Optional:** At this point, you can weigh your dough and divide it equally into 2 bowls, adding cocoa powder to one of the bowls to make a darker dough.

3 / Add the roughly chopped chocolate and nuts (if you have divided the dough as in step 2, then just divide the chocolate and nuts evenly between the

2 bowls. You can also add different types of chocolate and nut to each mixture for 2 very different types of cookies!). Mix until evenly combined. Use an ice-cream scoop to scoop the batter into balls. Don't smooth them out, just leave them rough. You can either scoop large cookies (about 80g [3oz] each), or smaller scoops (about 40g [1½oz]) for smaller cookies. Place the balls of dough onto the lined baking sheet, ensuring that there's a cookie-sized space around each ball of dough as they will spread out.

4 / Chill for 1 hour in the fridge. Just before they have finished their chilling time, preheat the oven to 210°C [400°F/Gas mark 6½].

Note: You can also freeze the scooped balls, and have a stash ready to be baked. They may just need a few extra minutes if baking from frozen.

5 / Once chilled, bake for 7–9 minutes for smaller cookies or 10–12 minutes for larger cookies. They should be brown on the edges and still soft in the centre. They will look underdone once baked, but they will firm up and continue to cook while they cool, so be careful not to overbake them! Leave them to cool on the baking sheets until they are firm enough to transfer to a wire rack to finish cooling.

6 / Once cool, colour the Royal Icing with food dyes, then transfer to piping [pastry] bags. Cut the tips of the bags or use a piping tip, then decorate the cookies with various festive faces. You can copy the examples here or create your own!

Vegan alternative

The vegan version, but I guarantee you won't be able to tell. Give them to your vegan and non-vegan friends alike!

MAKES: ABOUT 30 (40G [1½OZ] EACH) OR MAKE HALF THE NUMBER BUT JUMBO SIZE!

90g [6 Tbsp] coconut oil, at room temperature so it's soft and scoopable (you can use refined coconut oil if you don't want any coconut taste)
½ tsp salt
130g [⅔ cup] soft light brown sugar
85g [½ cup minus 1 Tbsp] caster or granulated sugar
1 tsp vanilla bean paste
160ml [⅔ cup] coconut milk
2 tsp baking powder
250g [2 cups minus 2 tsp] plain [all-purpose] flour (or use gluten-free flour plus 1 tsp xanthan gum)
1 Tbsp cornflour [cornstarch]
400g [14oz] vegan chocolate, roughly

chopped (half white and half dark, or experiment with what chocolate you add! See note about caramelized white chocolate, right)
150g [1 cup plus 1½ Tbsp] walnuts, toasted and roughly chopped (although you can use any nuts you like, or a combination of different nuts)

PLUS

add 20g [4 tsp] unsweetened cocoa powder to half the dough to create darker chocolate dough (optional)
food dyes of choice
sweets [candies]
edible eyes

To caramelize white chocolate: You need good-quality white chocolate for this. It needs to be over 30% cocoa butter for best results. Ideally you want to work with at least 400g [14oz] white chocolate, as you may as well make more (it will keep for other baking projects!), and you will want to snack on some. All you need to do is preheat the oven to 125°C [257°F/Gas mark ¼]. Line a shallow-rimmed baking sheet with baking paper, then roughly chop the chocolate and place it on the lined baking sheet. Place in the oven and leave for about 1 hour–1½ hours, stirring it every 15–20 minutes. The chocolate will go through phases of looking stiff and lumpy, but don't worry because after stirring it will become smooth again (as long as you keep checking on it regularly!). You will notice the chocolate gradually becoming more caramel coloured over time. Once it is a golden caramel colour, remove from the oven and transfer to another container, spread into a thin layer. Chill in the fridge for 1–2 hours or freeze for 10 minutes until solid again, then chop it up and use it in the above cookies (or any other recipe you like!).

1 / Place the coconut oil, salt and both sugars in a stand mixer fitted with a balloon whisk attachment (or use a handheld electric whisk) and whisk on high speed until light in colour. Add the vanilla and whisk again. Add the coconut milk and whisk until combined.

2 / Add the baking powder and both flours. Stir by hand until mostly mixed in but some flour is still visible (this is to avoid overmixing and overworking the gluten). Follow steps 2–6 of the main recipe above.

"Things may chip away at you, but unlike these delicious cookies, you won't crumble!"

Polar Bear Bombe

At first this may look like a daunting recipe, but when all the elements are broken down it is much more manageable. Ideally, give yourself 3 days for this, although you can prepare the joconde, syrup and crémeux on the first day, and then make the pâte à bombe mousse and assemble everything on the second day. On the final day, unmould, make the Italian Meringue Buttercream, decorate and serve! This technique for making the chocolate mousse may seem a little complex and will require a stand mixer, but it produces the most stable and incredibly delicious mousse you have ever tried! So is completely worth it.

SERVES: 8–10 (MAKES: 1 LARGE SHARING-SIZED CHOCOLATE BOMBE)

Note: You will have leftover mousse, Italian Meringue Buttercream and joconde, but you can make mini bombes with this and snack on them!

You will need a 20-cm [8-in] diameter semisphere mould (or a similar large bowl will do), plus a 10-cm [4-in] diameter bowl.

CARAMELIZED WHITE CHOCOLATE RASPBERRY CRÉMEUX
150g [5oz] caramelized white chocolate (see opposite, although this will still taste great with ordinary white chocolate!), finely chopped
1 medium egg yolk
20g [1½ Tbsp] caster or granulated sugar
1 tsp agar agar powder
100ml [7 Tbsp] whole milk
60ml [¼ cup] double [heavy] cream
3 tsp freeze-dried raspberry powder
pink gel food dye (optional)

JOCONDE
110g [3¾oz] egg whites
30g [2½ Tbsp] caster or granulated sugar
100g [1 cup] ground almonds
100g [¾ cup minus ½ Tbsp] icing [confectioners'] sugar
3 medium eggs
30g [3⅔ Tbsp] plain [all-purpose] flour (or use gluten-free flour)
25g [2 Tbsp] salted butter, melted and slightly cooled

SIMPLE SYRUP
50g [¼ cup] caster or granulated sugar
50ml [3½ Tbsp] water
2½ Tbsp amaretto/almond liqueur

PÂTE À BOMBE MOUSSE
600ml [2½ cups] double [heavy] cream
1 tsp almond extract
9 medium egg yolks
270g [1⅓ cups] caster or granulated sugar
70ml [4⅔ Tbsp] water
300g [10½oz] dark [bittersweet] chocolate (at least 70% cocoa solids), roughly chopped

PARTY HAT
100g [¾ cup minus ½ Tbsp] icing [confectioners'] sugar
25ml [2 Tbsp] water
1 ice-cream waffle cone
sprinkles

ITALIAN MERINGUE BUTTERCREAM
140g [¾ cup minus 2 tsp] caster or granulated sugar (divided in two)
pinch of salt
55ml [3⅔ Tbsp] water
55g [1¾oz] egg whites (about 2 medium)
⅛ tsp cream of tartar
170g [¾ cup] unsalted butter, at room temperature
vanilla bean paste

PLUS
flaked coconut
coloured fondant
gel food dyes
edible gold paint

1 / Make the crémeux first. Line a 10-cm [4-in] diameter bowl with plastic wrap. Put the chocolate in a large heatproof bowl. Using a balloon whisk, whisk the egg yolk, caster sugar and agar agar powder together in another large heatproof bowl until light. Heat the milk and cream over a medium-high heat until almost simmering, then gradually pour it into the egg mix, constantly whisking with a balloon whisk. Pour back into the pan and continue whisking over a medium-high heat until thickened and it coats the back of a spoon. Pour it over the chopped chocolate, leave for a minute, then add the raspberry powder and red food dye and stir until melted and combined. Immediately pour into the lined bowl and chill for a couple of hours, or overnight until set.

2 / To make the joconde, preheat the oven to 200°C [400°F/Gas mark 6]. Grease a 35 x 27-cm [14 x 10¾-in] shallow Swiss roll tin [jelly roll pan] with butter, then line the base with baking paper, allowing the paper to extend up 2 of the sides to help lift the cake out later. Whisk the egg whites in a stand mixer (or use a handheld electric whisk) fitted with the balloon whisk attachment to stiff peaks, then add the caster sugar, 1 Tbsp at a time, and whisk for 30 seconds after each addition, until all the sugar is incorporated and the mixture is firm and glossy. In a separate bowl, whisk the almonds, icing sugar and eggs together on high speed for 5 minutes until pale and doubled in volume. Sift in the flour and fold in until partially combined. Add the melted butter and fold in until combined. Gently fold in the egg whites in 3 stages. Pour into the prepared tin and bake for 8–10 minutes until the centre springs back when lightly touched.

3 / Meanwhile, for the simple syrup, add the sugar and water to a pan and heat over a high heat until all the sugar has dissolved. Reduce the heat and simmer for 1 minute, then remove from the heat and add the alcohol. Set aside. Lift the joconde (using the paper to help) onto a wire rack and poke holes over the surface with a skewer or chopstick. Brush with the simple syrup. Leave to cool. When cool, cut out a circle just smaller than your mould. Leave the remaining cake to cut out ears for decorating later!

4 / For the pâte à bombe mousse, whip the cream and almond extract in a stand mixer (or use a handheld electric whisk) fitted with the balloon whisk attachment to soft peaks. Chill in the fridge for now.

5 / Place the egg yolks in a stand mixer and whisk until fluffy and pale. Meanwhile, add the sugar and

water to a pan and heat over a high heat until it reaches 120°C [248°F] (try to time the egg yolks finishing whisking at a similar time to the sugar syrup reaching temperature – you can always slow the beaters if necessary). Pour the 120°C [248°F] sugar syrup onto the egg yolks while whisking on medium speed, then increase the speed to high and whisk until the bottom of the bowl is cool to touch: this is your pâte à bombe.

6 / Meanwhile, melt the chocolate in a heatproof bowl set over a pan of gently simmering water, making sure the base of the bowl doesn't touch the water. Once melted, leave the chocolate to cool to 40–45°C [104–111°F], then fold it into the cooled pâte à bombe. It will go quite thick and look uneven, but that's normal. Carefully fold in the almond cream in 3 stages, being careful not to knock out the air.

7 / For the party hat, make an icing by whisking the icing sugar and water together. Cover the surface of the waffle cone with the icing, then roll in the sprinkles to cover it completely. Leave to set.

8 / Make the Italian Meringue Buttercream following the instructions on page 32. Chill in the fridge for now.

9 / To assemble, line a 20-cm [8-in] semisphere bowl (or mould) with plastic wrap. Fill with mousse, but create a dip in the centre as you will be adding the crémeux and then the joconde. Peel the plastic wrap off the crémeux and place this in the centre of the mousse. Push down until all its sides are submerged in the mousse. Place the cake layer on top, allowing the mousse to cover its circumference. Chill in the fridge overnight until set.

10 / Once set, place a serving tray on top of the mould, then flip over. Remove the mould and peel off the plastic wrap. Cover with a thin layer of Italian meringue buttercream – don't worry about it being smooth as it will be covered with flaked coconut. Cut 2 semicircle ear shapes out of the joconde and stick on top in the buttercream. Cover the ears with more buttercream. Cover all the buttercream with flaked coconut. Use fondant to create the face, sticking it down with a little buttercream (you might need to wipe a small amount of the flaked coconut away to help it stick). Top with the set party hat, between the ears. Dye a small amount of the buttercream green (or colour of your choice) using gel food dye. Transfer to a piping [pastry] bag and pipe a buttercream border around the base of the hat using a decorative tip, then pipe a blob on the tip of the hat to finish.

Hot Chocolate Bombes

The addition of real melted chocolate in your hot chocolate, plus the ritual of placing the bombe in hot milk and watching it melt with the marshmallows and treats spilling out... it's everything Christmas is meant to be. Make a big batch of these, keep some for yourself, then package the rest to make personal gifts for friends and family.

You can make medium-sized bombes or even jumbo-sized ones! Put the same amount of powder into each, but you can fit extra marshmallows and treats in the jumbo-sized bombe, or add extra powder if it's for really large mugs of hot chocolate. You can experiment with what you add in, as well as different flavours of hot chocolate! Silicone moulds are the easiest to use for these: I use 4.7-cm [1¾-in] diameter moulds for smaller bombes, and 6.5-cm [2½-in] diameter moulds for jumbo-sized bombes, but any similar size will work well.

MAKES: AROUND 5 JUMBO-SIZED BOMBES, OR 10 MEDIUM-SIZED ONES (BUT FEEL FREE TO MAKE EXTRA FOR PRESENTS!)

TEMPERING
400g [14oz] white or dark [bittersweet] chocolate (it's easiest to work with this larger quantity when tempering as smaller amounts will experience quicker temperature changes! If you want to make both white chocolate and dark chocolate bombes, make a minimum 400-g [14-oz] batch of each. Any leftover chocolate can always be re-melted and reused later!)

FILLING
per bombe: 1 flat tsp unsweetened cocoa powder plus 1–2½ tsp sugar (depending on your taste)

per white chocolate bombe: add your favourite white hot chocolate mix according to packet instructions. You can also make a malt drink version!

PLUS
mini marshmallows and additional add-ins you would like! E.g. sprinkles, sweets [candy], chocolate chips
edible eyes
white icing (made from 200g [1½ cups minus 1 Tbsp] icing [confectioners'] sugar mixed with 30–45ml [2–3 Tbsp] water to make a pipeable consistency)
gel food dyes

It's best to temper your chocolate for these bombes, because if your chocolate is melted without tempering then it will take a long time to set, and it will be sticky and flexible rather than snap. The main issue is that it will be difficult to stick the 2 halves together as it will be melting from your warm fingers. Tempered chocolate cocoa bombes are also great for Christmas gifts, whereas untempered ones must be kept chilled or else they will go soft.

"Let those stresses melt away."

Can be made vegan!

1 / First, you will need to set up a bain-marie: sit a heatproof bowl (which is clean and completely dry) over a pan of simmering water (making sure the bottom of the bowl does not touch the water). Put three-quarters of the finely chopped chocolate into the heatproof bowl, and set aside a quarter of the chocolate for 'seeding' the chocolate later. Stir the chocolate until it has melted and its temperature is 43°C [109°F] for white chocolate or 46°C [115°F] for dark chocolate (you will need a thermometer). Start taking the chocolate off the heat before it reaches the desired temperature, because you will find that the temperature suddenly shoots up from the bowl, getting very hot. Add the remaining chunks of chocolate to the bowl, stirring constantly. Keep stirring until the temperature comes down to 28–29°C [82–84°F] for white chocolate or 32°C [90°F] for dark chocolate. Now your chocolate is tempered and ready to use. You can check it is tempered by leaving some to set on the back of a spoon. It should set within 5 minutes. Be careful not to let any water touch the chocolate, otherwise it will seize and become unusable. You can keep the chocolate slightly warm (but not beyond the tempered

temperature) in the bain-marie for a while, so you can use it when needed.

2 / Spoon the tempered chocolate into the silicone moulds and use the spoon to spread it around the sides to coat. Turn the mould upside down and shake to remove any excess chocolate (you don't want the shell to be so thick that you can't fit the filling in!). Chill in the freezer for about 5 minutes, or until set, then peel the chocolate from the silicone moulds – they should come out very easily once set.

3 / To assemble the basic bombe shape, first, warm a plate in the microwave. Place the rim of one of the chocolate semispheres on the plate until just slightly melted (you can wear gloves if you want to avoid fingerprints on the chocolate, although this isn't necessary), then fill this semisphere with your filling. Repeat the melting of the rim of the second semisphere and press both together to seal in the filling. You can leave this as it is or drizzle with more chocolate (make sure it isn't warm enough to melt the chocolate). Alternatively, you can create some of the character bombe shapes opposite.

STEP 2 ▼

CHRISTMAS PUDDINGS WITH EYES
Stick edible eyes onto a dark chocolate bombe using white icing, then drizzle white icing on top. Top with round red sprinkles and holly sprinkles. Chill in the fridge or freezer until completely set.

REINDEER
Pipe antlers using dark chocolate onto baking paper, then freeze for a few minutes. Attach to a dark chocolate bombe with more dark chocolate. Use a red sprinkle or chocolate for the nose (stuck on with extra chocolate or icing), then pipe details with icing and stick on edible eyes. Add edible glitter to the antlers, if liked. Chill in the fridge or freezer until completely set.

POLAR BEAR
Use extra chocolate or icing to add a marshmallow nose and ears to a white chocolate bombe, then pipe a face and eyes with icing. Chill in the fridge or freezer until completely set.

SNOWMAN WITH MELTING PUDDLE
Use a spoon to create a small puddle of white chocolate onto a piece of baking paper, then immediately place a white chocolate bombe on top. Add a hat using your favourite chocolates and pipe on a face using royal icing. Chill in the fridge or freezer until completely set.

Tip: You can also temper the chocolate in the microwave. Just use 15–30-second bursts to melt the chocolate to the specified temperature, then 'seed' with chocolate and cool in the same way as normal.

Christmas Kransekake

The *Kransekake* (in Norwegian) or *Kransekage* (in Danish) translates to 'wreath cake', and is a traditional treat eaten at celebrations such as New Year's Eve, Norway's Independence Day, and Christmas. It tastes very similar to marzipan, except that it's baked and deliciously chewy, so is perfect for all the marzipan fans out there. The whole process of shaping and baking all the rings and stacking them feels incredibly therapeutic. Don't worry if your rings aren't completely symmetrical and perfectly formed (as they do rise and crack a little in the oven); once they are all stacked and the decorations have been added it will look so impressive. Don't forget to add some candy and treats to the centre for a lovely surprise for your guests at Christmas!

> Can be made vegan!

SERVES: 30–50 (MAKES: 1 LARGE KRANSEKAKE)

GINGER AND ORANGE COOKIES

150g [⅔ cup] salted butter (or use vegan butter, at least 75% fat content)
120g [⅔ cup minus 2 tsp] dark muscovado [soft brown] sugar
¼ tsp salt (optional)
2 tsp black treacle [molasses]
2 Tbsp beaten egg (or aquafaba)
2 Tbsp ground ginger
¾ Tbsp ground cinnamon
¼ tsp ground cloves
finely grated zest of 1 orange
225g [1¾ cups] plain [all-purpose] flour, plus extra for dusting

ROYAL ICING

80g [3oz] egg white (or 80ml [⅓ cup] aquafaba)
400g [2¾ cups plus 1 tsp] icing [confectioners'] sugar
extra icing [confectioners'] sugar and egg white (or aquafaba) to adjust consistency for flood icing or outline
blue food dye

KRANSEKAKE

625g [4¼ cups plus 2 Tbsp] icing [confectioners'] sugar
625g [6¼ cups] finely ground almonds
5 medium egg whites
(to make vegan, substitute with 140ml [½ cup plus 4 tsp] aquafaba and 100g [¾ cup] plain [all-purpose] flour)
1 tsp vanilla bean paste
½ tsp almond extract

PLUS

edible glitter
candy or special present (optional)
sprinkles (optional)

1 / First, make the ginger and orange cookies. Line a baking sheet with baking paper. Place the butter, dark muscovado sugar, salt (if using) and treacle in a stand mixer fitted with a balloon whisk attachment (or use a handheld electric whisk) and whisk on medium speed until smooth and spreadable.

2 / Add the beaten egg (or aquafaba), the ginger, cinnamon, cloves and orange zest and mix until just combined.

3 / Add the flour and stir using a spatula until roughly combined. Using your hands, shape the dough into a ball. Turn out on to a lightly floured surface and roll out until it is 3mm [⅛in] thick. Use cutters or templates to cut out snowflake shapes (or any festive shapes you like) and transfer to the lined baking sheet.

4 / Chill the cookies in the fridge for at least 15 minutes. Preheat the oven to to 170°C [340°F/Gas mark 3] while you wait.

5 / Bake the cookies for 10–12 minutes until just beginning to colour. Leave to cool on the baking sheet for 10 minutes, before carefully transferring to a wire rack to cool completely.

6 / For the royal icing and decorating the cookies, place the egg white (or aquafaba) and icing sugar in a large bowl and whisk until you get a smooth consistency. Add tiny amounts of extra egg white (or aquafaba) and/or icing sugar to get a good piping consistency.

7 / Divide the royal icing between 2 bowls and add blue food dye to one of the bowls to colour as desired. Create a slightly thicker consistency for piping detailed lines and borders and a slightly runnier consistency for flooding (filling in between lines). You want the thicker consistency to hold a trail for about 10 seconds, although you can play about with slightly different consistencies. You will need to work faster with a thicker consistency, so this is better for small cookies such as the snowflakes, but they can also create a thicker icing with a 'puffy' appearance, which is nice as it looks more 3D.

8 / Place different colours/consistencies into different piping [pastry] bags and use to pipe snowflake designs (or any festive designs!) onto your cookies. Apply edible glitter using a paintbrush and gently dabbing on top of the icing. You can add the glitter while the icing is wet, or leave it to set completely before using a tiny amount of water to help the glitter stick. If piping is daunting for you, you can keep this simple by piping lines onto the snowflakes rather than solid areas of colour. Try to set some of the icing aside to assemble the kransekake later, although if you don't have any left then just make another batch.

9 / If you've covered large areas of the snowflakes with icing, then leave them to set for a few hours or preferably overnight. Setting time varies depending on humidity and how thick the icing has been piped. If you've just piped thin lines, this should set much quicker.

Royal icing can take a little while to get used to, but if you add lots of edible glitter you're sure to bring a smile to your friends' faces!

10 / For the kransekake, add the icing sugar, ground almonds, egg whites, vanilla and almond extract to a large bowl and use a spatula to mix together. It will seem like there isn't enough liquid at first, but keep mixing and it will come together. If you have a stand mixer, that helps speed things up and is easier as

this is a large quantity. The dough should feel a little sticky. Place it on a piece of plastic wrap to prevent it sticking to the work surface.

11 / Preheat the oven to 200°C [400°F/Gas mark 6] and line a baking sheet with baking paper or a silcone mat.

12 / You will need to create 18 rings from the kransekake dough. The smallest will be 10cm [4in] in circumference and the largest 53cm [21in], so you will need one 53cm [21in], one 50cm [20in], one 48cm [19in] and so on.

13 / To make a ring, pinch off a handful of dough (then wrap the rest of the dough in the plastic wrap to stop it drying out) and use the palms of your hands to roll it out into a long thin sausage shape, about 1–2cm [½–¾in] in diameter. You shouldn't need any flour to stop it sticking, but feel free to use some if it makes it easier. Use a knife to cut to your desired size, then press the ends together to form a circle (rub the edges with your finger to help seal) and place on the lined baking sheet. Be careful not to stretch the ring of dough out as you seal and lift it, as it could end up too large. Keep repeating until you've made all 18 rings of dough.

14 / You will need to bake these in several batches as they won't all fit on the sheet (especially not the larger rings) although you can fit some smaller rings within the larger with some clever arranging. If you have kransekake moulds, this makes it a lot easier as the rings won't become misshapen and you can bake more at once, but it's perfectly doable without the moulds. In the photograph on page 95, the rings were baked without any moulds! Bake for about 8–12 minutes until golden brown. Leave on the baking sheet to cool for 15 minutes, then transfer to a wire rack to finish cooling.

15 / To assemble the kransekake, have some white royal icing in a piping bag and blue royal icing in a second bag. Cut a tip on each to pipe from. Place the largest ring on a cake stand using a little icing to stick it down, then use the white icing to pipe a wiggly pattern across the top and down the sides a little (as the sides will be the part that's on display later). Repeat this with the blue icing, trying to pipe in the gaps of the white.

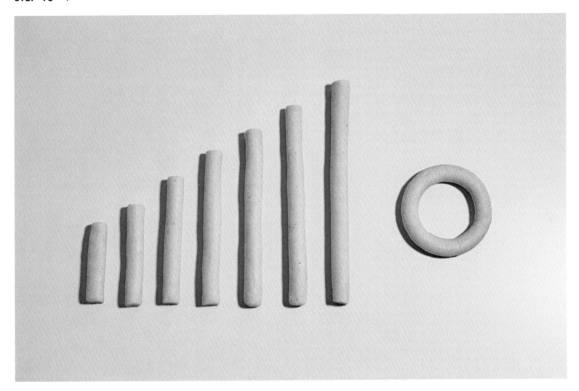

16 / Place the second largest ring on top (it should stick with the icing) and repeat. Keep going until you've added the smallest ring to the very top.

17 / You can then fill the centre with a surprise of your choice! Maybe add lots of candy or a special present. Use icing to stick the iced snowflake cookies all around and place one on top like the star atop a Christmas tree. You can also personalize it by adding sprinkles (stick with a little icing), edible glitter and any other decorations you like.

- CHRISTMAS -

Weddings

Space Turtle Croquembouche

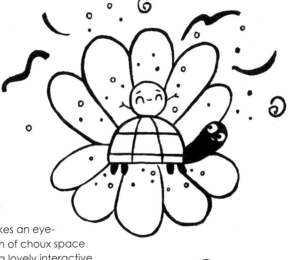

This classic French dessert is often served at weddings and makes an eye-catching centrepiece in its towering, golden form. The addition of choux space turtles make this into a fun and out-of-this-world bake, and it's a lovely interactive dessert for a wedding, as guests can break off the choux, piece by piece. Plus, as there are 2 different fillings (and you could even make more if you wanted to!) there's an added fun element of surprise as guests don't know which flavour choux they are picking up! You can make the choux au craquelin the day before, but it's best to fill and stack them on the day as the filling can make the choux soften over time.

"Shellebrate with Kim-Joy!"

MAKES: 1 LARGE SHARING-SIZED CROQUEMBOUCHE

CHOUX
(you need a big pan as it's a large amount)
275g [1¼ cups] unsalted butter
750ml [3 cups plus 2 Tbsp] water
pinch of salt
150g [1 cup plus 2 Tbsp] plain [all-purpose] flour
150g [1 cup plus 2 Tbsp] strong white flour (to make gluten free, substitute both flours with 300g [2¼ cups] gluten-free flour and ½ tsp xanthan gum)
9 medium eggs

CRAQUELIN
150g [⅔ cup] unsalted butter
150g [¾ cup] light muscovado [soft brown] sugar
150g [1 cup plus 2 Tbsp] plain [all-purpose] flour (or use gluten-free flour plus ¼ tsp xanthan gum)

COLOURED CRAQUELIN FOR THE TURTLE CHOUX
30g [2 Tbsp] butter
30g [2½ Tbsp] caster or granulated sugar
30g [3⅔ Tbsp] plain [all-purpose flour] (or use gluten-free flour plus ⅛ tsp xanthan gum)
gel food dyes in desired colours

CHOCOLATE ORANGE CRÈME DIPLOMATE
400ml [1⅔ cups] whole milk
grated zest of 2 oranges
1 tsp vanilla bean paste
7 large egg yolks
110g [½ cup plus 2 tsp] caster or granulated sugar
55g [½ cup] cornflour [cornstarch]
25g [2 Tbsp] unsweetened cocoa powder
175ml [¾ cup] double [heavy] cream

ALMOND & ORANGE LIQUEUR CRÈME DIPLOMATE
400ml [1⅔ cups] whole milk
grated zest of 2 oranges
1 tsp vanilla bean paste
7 large egg yolks
110g [½ cup plus 2 tsp] caster or granulated sugar
65g [⅔ cup] cornflour [cornstarch]
175ml [¾ cup] double [heavy] cream
50ml [3½ Tbsp] orange liqueur
¼ tsp almond extract (you can omit this if nut allergies are a concern!)

CARAMEL
675g [3⅓ cups] caster or granulated sugar
180ml [¾ cup] water

SECOND CARAMEL
675g [3⅓ cups] caster or granulated sugar
180ml [¾ cup] water

PLUS
almond halves
edible black pen or black food dye mixed with a small amount of vodka or alcohol-based extract
edible glitter

1 / Preheat the oven to 200°C [400°F/Gas mark 6] and line several baking sheets with baking paper or silicone mats (see Note under step 8).

2 / For the choux pastry, chop the butter and add it to a small saucepan with the water and salt. Heat until the butter has melted and the mixture is starting to bubble. Meanwhile, combine both flours in a separate bowl. When the butter mixture is bubbling, remove it from the heat and add the flours all in one go. Stir with a wooden spoon until it forms a smooth ball that pulls away from the sides very easily – this is called a panada.

3 / Transfer the panada to a stand mixer fitted with the paddle attachment (or use a handheld electric whisk) and leave to cool for 5–10 minutes.

4 / Meanwhile, make the craquelin for the choux. Cream the butter and sugar together in a large bowl until light and fluffy. Add the flour and combine with your hands to form a ball. Roll out between 2 sheets of plastic wrap, about 2mm [1/16in] thick, and transfer to the freezer. Repeat the same process for the coloured craquelin, except divide the dough into 3 and add food dye to each to colour as desired.

5 / Add 8 eggs, 1 at a time, to the panada, mixing on slow speed after each addition until combined. Whisk the final egg in a separate bowl and gradually add, 1 Tbsp at a time, mixing well after each addition. You are looking for a glossy consistency that leaves a 'v' shape when a spoon is lifted out of the dough.

6 / Transfer the choux pastry to a large piping [pastry] bag (not all the batter will fit, but it can be topped up later) and cut a medium tip (or use a large round piping tip). Pipe 20 x 3-cm [1¼-in] circles (these will form the body of the turtle), and then pipe much smaller circles for the heads (remember that these will double in size) onto the prepared baking sheets or mats. Insert 4 almond halves per turtle 'body', each one representing a leg. Remove the coloured craquelin from the freezer and use a round cutter to cut 20 x 3-cm [1¼-in] different-coloured circles, then top each choux 'body' with these.

7 / Bake for 10 minutes, then reduce the oven to 180°C [350°F/Gas mark 4] and bake for a further 20–25 minutes. Don't open the oven until at least 25 minutes have passed, to avoid the choux deflating. When the buns have finished baking, immediately turn them over and use a knife to pierce the base.

This is so that the air inside has somewhere to escape, and also gives you a place to pipe in the filling.

8 / For the plain choux au craquelin, pipe 3-cm [1¼-in] circles as before onto lined baking sheets (no need to add head and almonds this time), then top with craquelin in the same way as before, using the standard brown craquelin this time. Make sure that there is a gap between all the choux as they will double in size. Bake in the same way as before.

Note: You will need to pipe your choux (refilling the bag as you go along) on multiple baking sheets. If you trust your oven (you know it best), bake 2 sheets at a time, but it's perfectly fine to bake 1 sheet at a time as the choux can wait around before baking. However, add the craquelin just before you are ready to put the sheet in the oven, as the craquelin should be kept as cold as possible. Ideally, to ensure the craquelin is kept cold, stamp out all the circles in advance, return the circles to the freezer, then quickly place on the choux buns just before baking. You will need around 70–80 choux buns in total, so that will be 4–6 baking sheets, depending on the sizes of your sheets.

9 / Now make the chocolate orange crème diplomate. Put the milk, orange zest and vanilla bean paste into a medium saucepan and stir over a low-medium heat until just starting to bubble. Meanwhile, in a separate bowl, whisk the egg yolks and sugar until light and fluffy. Add the cornflour and cocoa powder and mix until just combined. When the milk mixture is bubbling, pour a small amount (about a third) into the egg yolk mixture, whisking constantly. When combined, add the rest of the milk while still whisking, then pour it all back into the saucepan.

10 / Put the pan back over a medium heat and whisk by hand until the mixture is very thick. Switch to a spatula when it becomes too thick to whisk, and use the spatula to get right into the edges of the pan. When the mixture is very thick, spoon this crème pâtissière into a shallow metal tray, cover with plastic wrap (making sure it touches the surface of the crème) and leave to cool in the fridge for 30 minutes.

11 / When the crème pat is completely cool, whip the double cream until it forms soft peaks, then gently fold into the crème. With the addition of the whipped cream to lighten it, you now have crème diplomate. Transfer to a large piping bag and cut a small-medium tip.

STEP 8 ▼

STEP 18 ▼

- WEDDINGS -

12 / Pipe the crème diplomate into half the cooled choux buns through the hole created earlier, making sure each one is filled completely. Set aside.

13 / Make the second crème diplomate in the same way, adding the liqueur and almond extract once the mixture is completely thickened, and just before leaving to cool. Pipe this into the remaining choux buns.

Note: You shouldn't combine the crème diplomate ingredients and make 1 larger batch. The large quantity will require a big pan and it's very hard to stir and cook evenly, so you are likely to get lumps! You can, however, play about with the flavours of the fillings and create your own. All these flavourings work very well: grated lemon zest, elderflower syrup, pistachio paste, yuzu, rose water, orange blossom water, freeze-dried fruits, lavender, coffee powder, liqueurs, matcha powder, praline paste and lots more.

14 / Finish the turtles by painting each turtles' facial features using an edible black pen or edible black food dye mixed with a little vodka and a paintbrush. Set these aside for now as they won't be topped with caramel.

15 / For the first batch of caramel, put the sugar and water into a large pan and heat over a high heat until golden in colour. Don't stir the caramel, as this will cause it to become grainy. You can also swirl the pan ever so slightly once the caramel starts to take on colour, just to make sure the colour is even throughout.

16 / Once the caramel is the desired colour, pour it into another bowl. Dip the choux, craquelin-side down and 1 at a time, into the caramel, twisting the bun so that the excess drips off. Place onto a sheet of baking paper, caramel-side facing up.

Note: You might need to wait a minute or two before dipping the first buns, as the caramel may be too hot and not provide a thick enough layer. Once you get started, work as quickly as possible while also being very careful not to burn yourself! Hot sugar sticks to your skin making the burn worse. If you're worried about burns from the sugar, wear thick gloves! You will find that as the sugar cools, it will become too

thick to dip easily. Before it gets to this point, give it a few seconds in the microwave (5–10-second bursts) and keep working. If the sugar gets grainy at any point, make another batch of caramel.

17 / Once all the choux have been dipped into the caramel, make the second batch of caramel in the same way. Use this caramel to stack all the choux. Arrange 12 choux around a 23-cm [9-in] diameter circle (you can use a template for accuracy in getting a perfect circle!), just to check that they fit, then dip the side of each choux into the caramel and use to stick them onto a serving tray with the caramel craquelin-side facing outwards. You may need to hold the choux in place for a few seconds, longer while the caramel is warmer.

18 / Repeat this process for the next layer up, sticking them to the choux buns beneath. Try to stick them in the gaps formed by the previous layer and angle them so they are pointing inwards ever so slightly, so that each layer becomes a smaller circle. Repeat with each subsequent layer, ending with just 2 choux buns on top.

19 / Place 2 turtles on the top and stick the remaining turtles to the outside of the croquembouche, arranging them so that they are flying in an arch and around the base as if they are holding up the croquembouche. Sprinkle with edible glitter.

20 / Finish by creating spun sugar. While dipping the choux buns in the caramel, you will have noticed that thin spun sugar strands were unintentionally created at certain points (this is when the caramel has cooled, but not cooled so much that it's hard). Now you want to get the caramel back to that magic temperature (you may need to zap it for a couple seconds in the microwave or leave it to cool a little more). Getting the temperature right is the hardest part, but once it's at the correct temperature (and you will get the feel for this after a while), dip a fork or (even better) a balloon whisk with the ends cut off with pliers into the sugar and move it rapidly around the croquembouche. If the caramel is the correct temperature, it will form spun sugar webs that will wrap round the croquembouche. Keep repeating until you're happy with the amount of spun sugar!

"Let negative vibes fly over your head."

Dragonfly & Geode Wedding Cake

If you're looking to make a wedding cake for someone, this is an excellent choice because the geode decoration is so simple yet effective. The best thing is that you can be tactical with where you carve the cake to disguise any bits of not-so-perfect fondant. You can also choose your favourite flavours for this – not all the tiers have to be same flavour! That way guests can have a selection to choose from. However, it's best to choose sturdier cakes for the base layers, such as the Vanilla Cake (page 10), Apple or Pear & Elderflower Cake (page 21) or the Ginger Cake (page 13). The more fragile cakes – Red Velvet (page 18), Chocolate (page 14), and Crème Brûlée (page 15) – are best for the top tier. If you're transporting this to a wedding, it's best to crumb coat and cover the individual tiers with fondant, then stack the whole cake and decorate it at the venue.

Can be made vegan!

SERVES 40–50 (MAKES: 1 LARGE WEDDING CAKE)

BASE TIER CAKE (22-CM [8½-IN])
2 quantities of any of the cakes on pages 10, 13 or 21. Don't just double the quantities in order to make the whole lot at once, as it will most likely be too much for your stand mixer/mixing bowls! Fill 2 x 22-cm [8½-in] cake tins per quantity, for a total of 4. You may need to adjust the baking time.

MIDDLE TIER CAKE (18-CM [7-IN])
1 quantity of any of the cakes on pages 10, 13 or 21

TOP TIER CAKE (15-CM [6-IN] TINS)
½ quantity of any of the tall cake recipes (pages 14, 15 or 18 work best). You may need to adjust the baking time.

BUTTERCREAM
2–3 quantities of American Buttercream (page 31) or Italian Meringue Buttercream (page 32)

PLUS
white fondant, about 2.3kg [5lb] for base tier, 1.9kg [4lb 3oz] for middle tier, 1.7kg [3lb 12oz] for top tier, plus extra fondant for shaping dragonflies
edible gold paint or gold lustre dust
vodka or alcohol-based extract
⅛ quantity of Royal Icing (page 94)
spring roll rice paper wrappers
blue, black, orange, pink gel food dyes
400g [2 cups] rock [candy] sugar
edible gold leaf

Tip: This is a large quantity of cake and a lot of work but it is for a wedding after all! If you want to make some cake in advance, just wrap in plastic wrap after cooling, and freeze. Leave to defrost partially before stacking. Cakes freeze really well and retain their moisture!

1 / First, make the dragonfly bodies. Shape a body using white fondant, then to give the dragonfly shape you can leave it to set on a curved silicone mat or similar, so that it sets in that shape. Once set (preferably overnight), paint it with edible gold paint (or mix gold lustre dust with a little alcohol to make a thick paint). Pipe 2 large eyes using white royal icing.

2 / For the dragonfly wings, see page 30 for how to make the rice paper spring roll sail shapes. Just use blue food dye with these and make them a little smaller – 4 for each dragonfly. Set overnight, then paint the edges and creases with edible gold paint.

3 / Make sure your 3 different cake tiers are cool before assembling. Stack and crumb-coat the cakes (see pages 27–28) using your chosen buttercream. Reserve some buttercream for the geode area later. Chill all the layers in the fridge until firm.

4 / Next, take a large piece of white fondant and roll it into a sausage. Now take a few smaller pieces of fondant that you've dyed different colours. Roll these out into long, thin sausages about the same length as the white fondant. Place on top of the white fondant, then twist a few times to start blending the colours together. You don't want to blend it too much! Roll out on a clean surface lightly dusted with cornflour or icing sugar, or use a thin coating of vegetable oil. Cover your rolling pin with the same. Roll out to a large circle, about 5mm [¼in] thick – it will need to be a lot bigger than your cake as it has to cover the top and sides! Pick it up by sliding your wrists and forearms underneath, then place on top of your cake. Use a fondant smoother tool to smooth the top over the cake, then work your way downwards,

pressing the fondant to the sides of the cake and pushing out any creases to ensure the fondant lays flat. At the base of the cake, use a sharp knife to cut off the excess. Use 2 smoothers at the same time just to get the edges neat and a little sharper. Don't worry if there are some issues with creases: you could incorporate these into the geode design later or cover with dragonflies. Repeat with all the tiers.

5 / Stack the cakes from largest to smallest (see pages 27–28), then carve a line where you want the geode to go. Once you're happy, use a sharp knife to cut out the fondant, then carve into the cake so that it has depth. Cover the exposed cake with some reserved buttercream, then stud this all over with rock sugar. Squeeze a dab of your chosen geode colours onto a plate, then paint onto the rock candy using a little bit of vodka (this evaporates faster and works better than water). Try to create a variety of shades and colours to look like natural rock. Paint edible gold paint around the edges and apply edible gold leaf to this so that it blends into the rest of the cake well.

6 / Use a little royal icing to attach the dragonflies onto the cake. Stick their wings into the fondant next to their bodies. Now pat yourself on the back!

STEP 4 ▼

Wedding 'Kitovai'

A 'korovai' is a traditional Ukranian, Polish and Russian sweet-tiered bread, usually made for weddings. It is traditionally decorated with unleavened dough which is made into ornate doves, flowers, suns, leaves and pine cones. This is my cat variation, perfect for couples who love cats – and I call it 'Kitovai' because 'kit' is Ukrainian for 'cat', although you can easily change the decorations to become whatever you like! Bunnies, dogs, snakes, birds… there are lots of possibilities. It's a great way to have something different at a wedding, and particularly for people who prefer bread to cake! The tangzhong technique is used in this bread, which helps to make the dough particularly soft and stay fresher for longer.

Tip: Use cake tins with removable bases to make it easier to get the bread out!

"Creativity from meowstakes is better than purrfection."

SERVES: AROUND 50

TANGZHONG
500ml [2 cups plus 2 Tbsp] water
125g [¾ cup plus 2 Tbsp] strong white flour, plus extra for dusting

KITOVAI-TIERED DOUGH
(this is a very large quantity of dough, so it helps to divide it into 2 more manageable quantities to work with)
grated zest of 4 oranges
grated zest of 3 lemons
625ml [2½ cups plus 2 Tbsp] whole milk
4 Tbsp vanilla bean paste
150g [⅔ cup] unsalted butter, melted
6 large eggs
400g [2 cups] caster or granulated sugar
25g [5 tsp] fine table salt
3 Tbsp ground cinnamon
1.75kg [12½ cups] strong white flour
4 x 7-g [¼-oz] sachets of fast-action dried [active-dry] yeast

400g [3⅓ cups] dried cranberries

DECORATIVE DOUGH
500g [3¾ cups] plain [all-purpose] flour
250ml [1 cup plus 2 tsp] water
80g [½ cup minus 4 tsp] caster or granulated sugar
gel food dyes in various colours (you can use green food dye or pandan paste for the green decorations)

red edible food paint or dye

PLUS
sunflower or other neutral-tasting oil, for oiling
2 eggs, beaten for egg wash
poppy or black sesame seeds
1 quantity of Royal Icing (page 94)
sprinkle pearls

1 / First, make the tangzhong. Using a balloon whisk, mix the water and flour together in a pan until smooth. Place the pan over a medium heat and stir constantly with a silicone or wooden spoon until thickened and it has reached 65°C [149°F] on a thermometer. Transfer to a small bowl, cover with plastic wrap (making sure this touches the surface of the tangzhong) and chill in the freezer for 10 minutes.

2 / Divide the grated lemon and orange zest between 2 stand mixers (or large bowls) so that you can work with the dough in 2 manageable quantities.

Add the following ingredients in the following order, but remember to divide between the 2 bowls: add the milk and vanilla and whisk by hand. Melt the butter in the microwave for 30 seconds and whisk in. Whisk in the eggs, then the sugar, salt and cinnamon. Remove the tangzhong from the freezer and add to the mix and mix this all by hand. Finally, add the strong white flour and put the yeast on top of this.

3 / Now you have 2 bowls, each with equal amounts of ingredients for dough. Let the stand mixer knead Dough 1 for about 10 minutes, or until smooth and

elastic. Place in a lightly oiled large glass bowl and cover with oiled plastic wrap. Repeat this process with Dough 2.

Note: You can also knead this by hand! It will just take a little longer. Stir the wet dough with a wooden spoon until the dough is shaggy, then tip onto your work surface and knead by hand. You can coat the work surface with a little oil to stop sticking, when needed. Also use a dough scraper to scrape up any dough that sticks to the surface.

MAKING THE DECORATIONS
4 / While the stand mixer is kneading Dough 2, start making the decorative dough. Just add the plain flour, water and sugar to a bowl, mix and knead until just combined. Tear off a quarter and add green food dye (or pandan paste) to colour.

5 / Leave Dough 1 to rise for 2 hours at room temperature until doubled in size and place Dough 2 in the fridge to slow its rise for about 8 hours, or until doubled in size. Alternatively, you can leave Dough 1 to rise in a very low oven (around 30°C [86°F]), and leave Dough 2 to rise at a cooler room temperature. You need to create different heat climates for each so that they rise at different rates!

Note: As you're working with a large amount of dough, you don't want it all to finish rising and leave you having to shape and bake it all at once (unless you have another person helping you and 2 ovens). To slow down the rise of any dough, cover it and pop it in the fridge – it will rise at a much slower rate.

6 / To make the decorations, shape 16 leaves using the green pandan-flavoured dough. Roll out the dough and use a knife to cut a leaf shape. Use the knife to lightly score the middle of the leaf and snip the edges with scissors. Paint on darker green lines using gel food dye mixed with a small amount of water.

7 / Roll out the remaining green decorative dough and use a knife or heart cutter to create the heart shape, then reroll the remaining dough and cut into 2 long thin strips. Make cuts along the length of one side and wrap around a long wooden skewer to create a 'vine'. Leave the bottom of the skewer exposed, as this will be pushed into the top tier.

8 / Shape 12 pink flowers with poppy seed centres: roll out about a third of the plain dough and use a

5-cm [2-in] metal cutter to get a round shape, then cut 5 petals. Use scissors to snip at the petals and create ruffled edges. Paint with pink food dye mixed with a tiny amount of water. Brush egg wash in the centre and sprinkle on some poppy seeds.

9 / Make 8 flower buds using the remaining plain dough. Cut long thin strips of dough using a pizza wheel, then gently roll over these once with the rolling pin to thin and roll up into rosebud shapes. Dip these into edible red food paint that has been mixed with a little water.

10 / Make 14 cats using the leftover plain dough in various shapes, colours and sizes (see the photo on page 109 for inspiration).

SHAPING THE BREAD TIERS
11 / Before shaping the bread, roll Dough 1 out on a lightly floured work surface, scatter with half of the cranberries, then roll up and knead until the fruit is evenly distributed. Shape Tier 1 using all of Dough 1, following these specifications: use about two-thirds of the dough to shape 9 balls of dough placed in the bottom of a greased 26-cm [10½-in] square cake tin. Shape the balls into smooth rounds. Use the last third of the dough for a braid, which will go on top and round the edge of the tin. Divide the dough into 2 equal pieces. Roll these on a lightly oiled surface until they are long and thin (long enough to wrap around the perimeter of the square tin), then twist them together. Wrap this braid around the entire outer edge of the tin, on top of the dough balls.

12 / Cover loosely with oiled plastic wrap and leave to rise at room temperature for 1 hour 30 minutes.

13 / Before shaping, roll Dough 2 out on a lightly floured work surface, scatter with the remaining cranberries, then roll up and knead until the fruit is evenly distributed. Use about two-thirds of the dough to shape the second tier, setting aside the remaining third for the top tier. Use three-quarters of this dough to shape 6 balls of dough placed in the bottom of a greased 23-cm [9-in] round cake tin, as you did for Tier 1. With the remaining quarter of the dough, divide it in 2 and make a braid as for Tier 1. Place this around the edge of the tin. Cover with oiled plastic wrap and place in the fridge to slow down the rise.

14 / Use the remaining dough set aside for Tier 3. Divide into 4 balls, then place in the base of a greased 15-cm [6-in] round cake tin. The dough should only come halfway up the tin. If there is extra, shape it into circles and bake separately to snack on. Cover with oiled plastic wrap and refrigerate.

15 / Your dough will all rise at different rates. If any are rising too fast and can't be baked yet, place in the fridge to slow the rising down. After you've followed the steps below for decorating and baking each tier below, you'll need to bake all the tiers at 180°C [350°F/Gas mark 4]. Tiers 1 and 2 are large breads, so it can help to check the internal temperature (it should be at least 93°C [199°F]) to check if they are baked in the centre. You can remove the breads from the cake tins immediately (run a knife around the edges and the removable bases can just be pushed upwards to reveal the sides of the bread). Leave to cool on a wire rack. Here are the instructions for decorating and baking each individual tier (once it's risen to double its size).

TIER 1

16 / Brush Tier 1 with egg wash and arrange the decorations. Per corner: 2 leaves, 1 rosebud and 1 flower. Arrange 8 cats and add some flowers. There isn't a precise place to add these, just make sure they are near the outer edge of the dough. Due to their weight, the cats will move a bit as the bread has its initial oven spring, so take this into account. Bake for 50 minutes. Set a timer for 20 minutes to check on the bread and how brown it is. It will probably

take 20–30 minutes to achieve the optimum level of browning. Tent with foil once it does achieve the right colour to prevent it browning further.

Tiers 2 and 3 can be baked together as both should fit in the oven and are smaller than Tier 1.

TIER 2

17 / Arrange 4 flowers, 4 leaves, 4 rosebuds and 4 cats around the edge. This tier will take around 40 minutes to bake. Keep an eye out for when it has browned enough, then tent with foil.

TIER 3

18 / Place 2 larger cats in the middle of the dough with the small green heart in front of them. Bake for about 25 minutes.

19 / When the tiers are out of the oven and cooling, bake the 2 green vines and the remaining decorations for about 20 minutes. Stack all the tiers on a stand and add the last details. Put the coloured sprinkle pearls between some of the cat paws to represent a ball. Use Royal Icing to attach the remaining extra decorations on the sides of the bread dough. Push the 2 vines into the top tier and hang bunting or a banner between them. You could make a personalized banner that says something special about the happy couple getting married! Or should it be getting 'meowwied'?

Graduation: Orange & Dark Chocolate Choux People

A graduation ceremony is a culmination of so much hard work, it deserves to be celebrated with deliciously cute choux buns, which, thankfully, are not as much work as hours and hours of studying for exams and writing essays! You can customize the design to match the graduate's gown, or their favourite colours.

MAKES: 20–24

CHOUX PASTRY
85g [⅓ cup plus 2 tsp] unsalted butter
225ml [1 cup minus 1 Tbsp] water
pinch of salt
50g [6 Tbsp] plain [all-purpose] flour
50g [5¾ Tbsp] strong white flour
2–3 medium eggs

ORANGE CRAQUELIN
75g [⅓ cup] unsalted butter
75g [6 Tbsp] light muscovado [soft brown] sugar
finely grated zest of 1 orange
75g [½ cup plus 1 Tbsp] plain [all-purpose] flour

ORANGE BLOSSOM CRÈME DIPLOMATE
400ml [1⅔ cups] whole milk
finely grated zest of 1 orange
¾ tsp vanilla bean paste
7 large egg yolks
90g [½ cup minus 2 tsp] caster or granulated sugar
60g [⅔ cup] cornflour [cornstarch]
1 Tbsp orange blossom water
170ml [¾ cup minus 2 tsp] double [heavy] cream

MARZIPAN (OR USE STOREBOUGHT)
125g [¾ cup plus 2 Tbsp] icing [confectioners'] sugar, plus extra for dusting
125g [1¼ cups] finely ground almonds
1 pasteurized egg white (or 35g [1¼ oz])
¼ tsp almond extract
¾ tsp amaretto
gel food dye (to match the colour of graduation gown you want)

DARK CHOCOLATE HATS
400g [2¾ cups] dark [bittersweet] chocolate (at least 70% cocoa solids), finely chopped (this is a large quantity as it is easier to temper, although you can re-melt and reuse it for another baking project)
OR
150g [1 cup] black or brown candy melts (these won't need tempering, but won't taste nearly as good as real chocolate!)

PLUS
jam of choice
edible black pen or black food dye mixed with a small amount of vodka or alcohol-based extract
sweets [candy], to decorate tops of hats
flaked [slivered] almonds

---

1 / Preheat the oven to 200°C [400°F/Gas mark 6]. Line 2 baking sheets with baking paper or a silicone mat.

2 / For the choux pastry, chop the butter and add it to a small pan with the water and a pinch of salt. Heat until the butter has melted and the mixture is starting to bubble. Meanwhile, combine both flours in a separate bowl. When the butter mixture is bubbling, remove it from the heat and add the flours all in one go. Stir with a wooden spoon until it forms a smooth ball that pulls away from the sides very easily – this is called a panada.

3 / Transfer the panada to a stand mixer fitted with the paddle attachment (or use a handheld electric whisk) and leave to cool for 5–10 minutes.

4 / Meanwhile, make the orange craquelin. Cream the butter and sugar together in a large bowl until light and fluffy. Add the orange zest and mix. Add the flour and combine with your hands to form a ball. Roll out between 2 sheets of plastic wrap, about 2mm [¹⁄₁₆in] thick, and transfer to the freezer.

5 / Add 2 eggs, 1 at a time, to the panada, mixing on slow speed after each addition until combined. Whisk the third egg in a separate bowl and gradually add 1 Tbsp at a time, mixing well after each addition. You are looking for a glossy consistency that leaves a 'v' shape when a spoon is lifted out of the dough.

6 / Transfer to a piping [pastry] bag and cut a medium tip. Pipe 20 x 3-cm [1¼-in] circles onto one of the prepared baking sheets. Remove the craquelin from the freezer and cut out 20 x 3-cm [1¼-in] circles, then top each choux bun with these.

7 / Bake for 10 minutes, then reduce the oven to 180°C [350°F/Gas mark 4] and bake for a further 20–25 minutes. Don't open the oven until at least 25 minutes have passed, to prevent the choux deflating.

8 / While the choux are baking, pipe a second batch onto the other prepared baking sheet. This time you will need 20 x 2-cm [¾-in] circles. Top each with a similarly sized disc of craquelin (there will be some leftover choux so you can pipe extra if desired).

9 / When the first batch of buns have finished baking, immediately turn them over and use a knife to pierce the base. This is so that the air inside has somewhere to escape, and also gives you a place to pipe in the filling. Bake the second batch of choux buns for 10 minutes at 200°C [400°F/Gas mark 6], then a further 10 minutes at 180°C [350°F/Gas mark 4].

10 / While the choux are baking, make the orange blossom crème diplomate. Put the milk, orange zest and vanilla bean paste into a medium pan and stir over a low-medium heat until just starting to bubble. Meanwhile, in a separate bowl, whisk the egg yolks and sugar until light and fluffy. Add the cornflour and mix until just combined. When the milk mixture is bubbling, pour a small amount (about a third) into the egg yolk mixture, whisking constantly. When combined, add the rest of the milk while still whisking, then pour it all back into the saucepan.

11 / Put the pan back over a medium heat and whisk by hand until the mixture is very thick. Switch to a spatula when it becomes too thick to whisk, and use the spatula to get right into the edges of the pan. When the mixture is very thick, take the pan off the heat and stir in the orange blossom water. Place back over the heat for a few seconds while stirring constantly to thicken again. Spoon into a shallow metal tray or bowl, cover with plastic wrap (making sure it touches the surface of the crème) and leave to cool in the fridge for 30 minutes–1 hour 30 minutes. If you have any lumps in your crème pat, you can strain it before chilling.

12 / When the crème pat is completely cool, whip the double cream until it forms soft peaks, then gently fold into the crème. It may help to whisk the crème pat first just to loosen it a bit. With the addition of the whipped cream to lighten it, you now have crème diplomate. Transfer to a piping bag and leave in the fridge until ready to use.

13 / Pipe the crème diplomate into the cooled choux buns through the hole created earlier, making sure each one is filled completely. Set aside.

14 / For the marzipan, mix the dry ingredients together in a bowl and whisk the wet ingredients, except the food dye, together in a separate bowl. Add the wet to the dry and stir until just starting to combine. Knead on a work surface lightly dusted with icing sugar until it becomes smooth and forms a ball.

15 / Add food dye to your marzipan and knead until the colour is evenly distributed. You can create different colours, if you like.

16 / On a work surface lightly dusted with icing sugar, roll the marzipan out thinly and cut out 20 circles, about 6cm [2½in] in diameter, then place one on top of each larger choux bun using a dot of jam to make it stick. Place the smaller choux bun on top, using a dot of jam to help it stick. Use an edible black pen or black food dye mixed with a little vodka to draw in eyes and a dot for the mouth.

17 / Temper the dark chocolate (page 92) or use candy melts. Smooth the chocolate over acetate (or baking paper) and leave to set. Cut the set chocolate into 3-cm [1¼-in] squares, then place a small chocolate square on top of each choux bun and secure with a little jam or extra melted chocolate. Place a sweet on top of the chocolate to resemble a graduation hat, then insert almond halves into the sides to create arms.

Mother's & Father's Day: Panda Doughnuts

Soft, fluffy deep-fried doughnuts are not what you might first think of for Mother's and Father's day, but they are perfect because a good doughnut is like a big comforting hug. Plus the doughnut centre and ring fit together perfectly, just like great families do.

Note: Make either the dairy-based dough or the vegan dough following the appropriate method below.

Can be made vegan!

MAKES: ABOUT 10–12 RING DOUGHNUTS AND 10–12 DOUGHNUT HOLES

DAIRY-BASED DOUGH

375g [2⅔ cups] strong white flour
40g [3¼ Tbsp] caster or granulated sugar
8g [½ Tbsp] salt
10g [⅓oz] fast-action dried [active-dry] yeast
grated zest of ½ lemon or ½ orange (optional)
60ml [¼ cup] water
55ml [3⅔ Tbsp] whole milk
3 large eggs

80g [⅓ cup] unsalted butter, softened at room temperature

VEGAN TANGZHONG PASTE

100ml [⅓ cup plus 1 Tbsp] water
25g [2¾ Tbsp] strong white flour

VEGAN DOUGH

75ml [5 Tbsp] sunflower or other neutral-tasting oil, plus extra for oiling

2 Tbsp aquafaba
90ml [6 Tbsp] soy milk
40g [3¼ Tbsp] caster or granulated sugar
8g [½ Tbsp] salt
275g [2 cups] strong white flour, plus extra for dusting
12g [½oz] fast-action dried [active-dry] yeast

GLAZE

300g [2 cups plus 2 Tbsp] icing [confectioners'] sugar, plus a little extra

45–75ml [2–3 Tbsp] lemon juice
white food dye (optional, though helps make the icing more opaque)
1 tsp unsweetened cocoa powder
black food dye

PLUS

oil, for deep-frying
mini chocolate buttons
sprinkles, edible flowers, fondant or more icing

DAIRY-BASED DOUGH

1a / If working by hand, add the flour, sugar, salt, yeast and grated zest (if using) to a large bowl and stir for a few seconds to distribute the ingredients evenly.

2a / In a separate bowl, whisk the water, milk and eggs together. Add the liquid ingredients to the dry, and use a spoon to combine until you achieve a rough dough. Tip out the dough onto your work surface and knead until smooth and elastic.

3a / Gradually add the butter (40g [3 Tbsp] at a time) and knead in. The dough may stick to the work surface but it is important to avoid adding any extra flour. Use a dough scraper to clean the work surface as you go along.

1b / If you have a bread machine or stand mixer fitted with the dough hook attachment, simply add all the dry ingredients, mix, then add all the wet ingredients, except the butter. Let the machine knead the dough until smooth and elastic, about 7 minutes, then add the butter and let the machine knead this in for a further 5 minutes.

"Doughnut give up!"

VEGAN DOUGH

1 / First, make the tangzhong paste. Using a balloon whisk, mix the water and flour together in a pan until smooth. Switch to a spatula, and continue to stir over a medium heat until thickened to a pudding-like consistency and it has reached 65°C [149°F]. Pour into a bowl, cover with plastic wrap (make sure this touches the surface of the tangzhong) and chill in the freezer for 10 minutes.

2 / Meanwhile, add the oil, aquafaba, soy milk, caster sugar and salt to a large bowl or stand mixer if you have one. Add the chilled tanghong to the bowl and whisk together (the oil will separate – this is normal and expected), then add the flour and yeast.

3a / If using a stand mixer, just allow the machine to knead for 10 minutes with the dough hook attachment.

3b / If working by hand, use a wooden spoon to combine everything into a shaggy ball of dough, then turn out onto a floured surface and knead by hand for about 10–15 minutes. The dough will be sticky to start with, but avoid adding too much flour – it will gradually become less sticky as you knead it. If the dough sticks to the surface, use a dough scraper to scrape it off. Keep kneading until the dough is smooth; it will still be a little tacky but that is normal.

4 / Now take your dairy-based or vegan dough, place it in a lightly oiled large bowl and cover with plastic wrap. Leave to rise until doubled in size. This might take around 2–3 hours at room temperature.

Tip: You can speed up the rise by placing the covered dough in the oven preheated to a very low temperature (about 30°C [86°F]).

5 / When the dough has risen, knock it back and roll out on a lightly floured surface until about 2cm [¾in] thick. The dough will keep trying to shrink back every time you roll it out, so let it relax and shrink back a little, then roll it out again to get the desired thickness. Make sure the dough is relaxed and not still shrinking back before you start to stamp out the doughnut shapes. This will help you to get even and round shapes. If the dough is still trying to shrink back, then the doughnuts will be misshapen.

6 / Stamp out 10–12 circles (I use an 8-cm [3¼-in] cutter) and carefully transfer each of these to an individual square of baking paper. Once transferred,

you can cut out the centres (I use a 3-cm [1¼-in] cutter). Removing the centres after transferring to baking paper helps to make sure that each ring doughnut is even in size and shape.

7 / Reroll the dough to stamp out as many doughnuts as possible. Set the doughnut holes on individual baking paper squares as well. Loosely cover all the doughnuts with lightly oiled plastic wrap.

8 / Leave to rise for about 1–2 hours (depending on room temperature) until doubled in size.

9 / Heat enough oil for deep-frying in a large, deep, heavy-based pan to 180–185°C [356–365°F], and try to maintain this temperature while frying the doughnuts. Fry about 3 doughnuts at a time, carefully lowering them into the oil along with the baking paper underneath (this helps to keep the doughnuts shape and not deflate during transfer). Use tongs or a similar utensil to remove the baking paper from the oil as quickly as possible. Fry all the doughnuts for 45 seconds on each side.

10 / When the doughnuts have been fried on both sides, remove from the oil with a slotted spoon and drain on paper towels. After the oil has been soaked up, you can coat these in sugar straightaway (they are irresistible when still warm from the pan), or you can decorate them as parent and baby pandas before eating!

TO DECORATE

11 / Make the glaze by whisking the icing sugar and lemon juice together in a bowl until smooth. You want the icing to cover the doughnut well, but not be too thin that it drips all the way down the sides. Add a little white food dye to get a more opaque colour (optional but it does help).

12 / Dip the doughnuts (rings and doughnut holes) into the white glaze until evenly covered. Use a finger to smooth the icing that tries to drip down the side. Stick the doughnut hole in the centre of the ring doughnut, then press in chocolate buttons for the ears and leave until semi-set. Add enough extra icing sugar plus the 1 tsp cocoa powder to the glaze to make a thick pipeable consistency, then add black food dye to colour black. Transfer to a piping [pastry] bag and use to pipe both the pandas' facial details. You can customize the doughnuts to resemble you and your mother/father! Use sprinkles, edible flowers, fondant or more icing.

New Home: Gingerbread House

This is a very customizable recipe in terms of decoration – and this sturdy yet tasty cookie recipe will help you on your way to putting your own touch on it so that it resembles the new home that the lucky recipient is moving into! You can make a fantasy version with lots of bright colours and candy for decoration just like the one pictured here, or you could go down a more realistic route and use colours to match the actual house. With all the effort and creativity that goes into this, the new homeowner will be delighted no matter what the end result is. It's also perfect to nibble on as they settle in to their new home.

> Can be made vegan!

MAKES: 1 LARGE GINGERBREAD HOUSE TO SHARE

GINGERBREAD STRUCTURE
3 quantities of Ginger and Orange Cookie dough (page 94)
plain [all-purpose] flour, for dusting

MARZIPAN (OR USE STOREBOUGHT)
(you will need 750g [2½ cups] of marzipan so you will need to multiply this recipe by 3, or use store-bought if you prefer)
125g [¾ cup plus 2 Tbsp] icing [confectioners'] sugar, plus extra for dusting
125g [1¼ cups] ground almonds
1 egg white (or 40ml [2⅔ Tbsp] aquafaba to make vegan)
¼ tsp almond extract
¾ tsp amaretto

Note: If you prefer, you can use fondant instead of marzipan!

CARAMEL GLUE
250g [1¼ cups] caster or granulated sugar
50ml [3½ Tbsp] water

ROYAL ICING
see page 94

CHOCOLATE POPCORN TREES
(makes 3 large trees, although you could make more smaller trees)
100g [3½oz] brown candy melts OR white candy melts dyed brown using oil-based food colouring OR tempered dark chocolate (page 92)
45g [7 cups] popped popcorn
200g [7 oz] green candy melts OR white candy melts dyed green using oil-based food colouring OR tempered white chocolate (page 92) dyed green using oil-based food colouring

TO DECORATE
(you can pick and choose which elements you make and maybe make some of your own!)
candy floss, for the bushes
dyed fondant, for the fondant plants (page 41)
pink wafer cookies, for the roof
¼ quantity of Chocolate Cake (page 14) or Vegan Chocolate Cake (page 25), baked and cooled, for the soil
3 x pale/beige-coloured cookies plus ½ tsp matcha powder, for the green soil
edible flowers or fondant flowers

rice paper spring roll wrapper shapes (page 30), twig-shaped pretzels (or similar) and yellow, orange and red gel food dyes, for the fire
pretzel sticks and orange fondant, for the vegetable patch
1 mini pink marshmallow and black royal icing, for the pig
2 white marshmallows, pink fondant and black royal icing, for the panda
various sweets [candy], iced cookies and sprinkles

PLUS
2 tsp jam, for covering the house
gel food dyes
edible black pen (optional)

1 / First, make some paper or card templates for your cookie house. This is a lot simpler than it sounds! For the shape shown in the photograph on page 120, you will need 6 panels altogether, but each one is cut around twice, so only 3 different templates need to be made. Start by drawing the front/back of the house panel, using a ruler to make it straight. When you break it down, it's simply a rectangle with a triangular shape above. Cut this shape out.

2 / Now you need to make a panel for the 2 sides of the house. Make this the same height as the vertical edge on the front/back house panel, and use your eye to keep the length in proportion. If you cut this panel out and hold it together you should get an idea of how it all fits, then you can trim and adjust as needed. Finally, create the panel for the roof. One side needs to be a little bit longer than the side panel (to account for cookie thickness!), and the other side needs to a little bit longer than the slope on the front/back panel because you will want some overhang. Once you have all your panels and you're happy with them, you can use them to cut out your cookie shapes. You don't have to create this shape – try experimenting with different shapes to resemble the new home!

3 / Next, take the Ginger and Orange cookie dough and roll a third of it over a large sheet of lightly floured baking paper, using a little additional flour on top to prevent it sticking. Roll it out to about 3mm [⅛in], then using a pizza wheel or a sharp knife, cut out as many panels as you can fit (you will need to cut out 2 from each shape). Remove the excess dough around the cut-outs, then slide a baking sheet under the baking paper. This technique means that you don't need to transfer the cut shapes to a baking sheet, which would likely result in a slight distortion of the shape! Repeat, rolling out a third of the dough at a time, until you have all 6 panels.

4 / Chill the dough in the fridge for at least 15 minutes, or freeze for 10 minutes. While you wait, preheat the oven to 170°C [340°F/Gas mark 3].

5 / Bake the panels for about 15 minutes, or until starting to darken around the edges. Remove from the oven and leave to cool on the baking sheet for 15 minutes, or until firm, then transfer to a wire rack to finish cooling.

Tip: Once the cookies are baked, if there are any edges that have become wonky, you can trim them while they're hot.

6 / If you are making the marzipan, stir the icing sugar and ground almonds together in a large bowl. Add the egg white (or aquafaba), almond extract and amaretto to a separate large bowl and stir together, then stir into the dry ingredients until it is just starting to combine. Knead on a work surface lightly dusted with icing sugar until smooth and forms a ball, then roll out to about 3mm [⅛in] thick. Use the same templates again to cut out marzipan shapes to fit on the panels. There's no need to add marzipan to the roof if you're covering it with cookies or similar.

7 / Spread a little bit of jam on the panels you want to stick the marzipan to, then press the marzipan on top until it sticks.

8 / Next, make the caramel glue, which will hold the house together. Add the sugar to a large pan (it needs to be big enough for dipping the sides of the panels in), then pour over the water to hydrate the sugar. Heat over a high heat without stirring until the caramel becomes golden in colour. When it starts to take colour, you can swirl the pan a tiny bit to even out the colour, but you shouldn't need to do this much. Once the caramel is golden brown, remove it from the heat. Work quickly to dip the sides of the panels into the caramel and use to stick them to each other, holding for a few seconds until the caramel hardens.

Tip: Make sure you are assembling the panels directly on your chosen serving tray, because it is likely the caramel will glue itself to the base as well. You want to start with the base structure, then add the roof last. You will need to hold the panels together a little bit longer when the caramel is hotter, but as it cools you will find that it sticks faster. If you're working with a bigger or more complicated structure than this, pour the caramel into a heatproof bowl before dipping. If left in the hot pan for too long, it will continue to caramelize and brown. If the caramel becomes too firm to dip, just pop it into the microwave for 15 seconds.

TO DECORATE

9 / Cut out marzipan shapes for the windows and front doors, adding food dye to colour them however you like.

10 / Colour the Royal Icing as desired and use this to decorate the windows, doors and anything else you would like to add. (See page 96 for tips for piping.)

11 / Stick the marzipan pieces on using a little extra icing, then decorate with candy, sprinkles and cookies using royal icing to make everything stick. Create little bushes using candy floss. The pink wafer roof is made by splitting pink wafers into layers, then cutting them into smaller rectangles and layering them on the roof using royal icing to stick. You can make the roof using different cookies, or use marzipan or fondant-layered shapes for a more realistic look, if liked.

12 / Take the baked and cooled Chocolate Cake and crumble it up to create the soil. Crush the cookies either in a food processor or place in a bag and bash with a rolling pin. Colour green by stirring through the matcha powder. You can sprinkle this on top of the chocolate cake 'soil' for added interest, then decorate with edible flowers, fondant flowers and any additional ideas you have!

13 / For the bonfire, see page 30 for how to make rice paper spring roll wrapper shapes. Make them small and colour with a gradient of yellow, orange and red. Once set, arrange in a little pile of pretzels (or similar) to look like a bonfire.

14 / The vegetable patch is chocolate cake crumbs in a border of pretzel sticks with little orange fondant carrots and a miniature pig made from a mini pink marshmallow and details piped on using royal icing or an edible black pen. The panda is made from 2 white marshmallows stacked on top of each other with details piped on using black royal icing and a pink fondant party hat. Feel free to add lots more additions! Make creatures and/or people out of fondant or bake a few more cookies from the leftover dough and use royal icing to decorate these as desired!

15 / For the chocolate popcorn trees, melt brown candy melts in the microwave in 15–30-second bursts (longer initially, then shorter bursts afterwards), stirring well after each, OR temper dark chocolate (page 92). Transfer to a piping [pastry] bag, cut a small tip and use to pipe the shape of 3 tree trunks (about 12cm [4½in] long) onto baking paper. Leave to set at room temperature, or chill in the fridge or freezer.

16 / Place the popcorn in a large bowl. Melt the green candy melts in the microwave in 15–30 second bursts (longer initially, then shorter bursts afterwards), stirring well after each. OR temper white chocolate (page 92), then add oil-based green food dye to colour. Once melted, pour over the popcorn and mix until all the popcorn is coated, then spoon the popcorn onto the tree trunks, covering the top of them so it all sticks together. While the mixture is still wet, place sweets on top to resemble fruits or flowers. Leave to set at room temperature or chill in the fridge or freezer.

17 / Once set, you can peel the tree easily off the baking paper. It won't be able to stand up on its own, but you can lean it against the house or against a backing board as part of the scene.

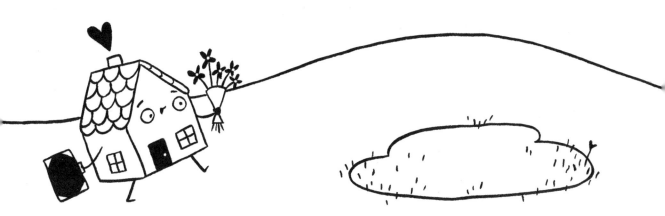

April Fool's Day: Chicken & Chips Illusion Cake

Prepare this savoury-looking meal to trick your friends and family – they may even prefer this version to real chicken and chips! The chocolate cake pop 'chicken' tastes extremely decadent, plus you can store the pops in the fridge and they should keep for a while, as the buttercream and chocolate coating prevents the cake from drying out. The shortbread chips melt in your mouth (just make sure you don't overwork the dough!) with an orange flavour that pairs perfectly with the salted caramel 'ketchup'. It will taste amazing but befuddle your brain all at the same time.

Can be made vegan!

SERVES: 3–5 (MAKES ABOUT 12 DRUMSTICKS AND 3 PORTIONS OF CHIPS)

BUTTERCREAM
80g [⅓ cup plus 1 tsp] butter (or vegan butter, must be at least 75% fat content)
1 tsp vanilla bean paste
160g [1 cup plus 2 Tbsp] icing [confectioners'] sugar
½ Tbsp whole milk (skip this if making vegan)
2 Tbsp unsweetened cocoa powder

CAKE POP CHICKEN
½ quantity of Chocolate Cake (page 14) or

Vegan Chocolate Cake (page 25), baked in 2 x 18-cm [7-in] tins and cooled

CARAMEL KETCHUP
(this makes extra but you can store it in a jar and enjoy later)
90ml [6 Tbsp] water
240g [1¼ cups minus 2 tsp] caster or granulated sugar
225ml [1 cup minus 1 Tbsp] double [heavy] cream or coconut milk
fine table salt, to taste
red food dye

SHORTBREAD CHIPS
200g [¾ cup plus 2 Tbsp] salted butter (or use vegan butter, at least 75% fat content for best results)
85g [½ cup minus 1 Tbsp] caster or granulated sugar
1 Tbsp vanilla bean paste
grated zest of 2 oranges
270g [2 cups] plain [all-purpose] flour (or gluten-free flour plus ¾ tsp xanthan gum), plus extra for dusting

PLUS
12 cake pop sticks
170g [6¾ cups] cornflakes or similar
granulated sugar for sprinkling
300g [1¾ cups] white chocolate, roughly chopped OR use yellow candy melts
yellow oil-based food dye (or cocoa butter)

1 / For the buttercream, put the butter, vanilla and icing sugar in a stand mixer fitted with a balloon whisk attachment (or use a handheld electric whisk) and whisk on slow speed until the sugar is combined (you may want to cover the bowl with a tea towel [dish towel] to prevent the icing sugar flying everywhere!).

2 / Increase the speed to high and whisk until light and fluffy, scraping down the sides of the bowl with a spatula to ensure everything mixes properly. Whisk in the milk (no need if making vegan) to achieve a spreadable consistency. Remove 2 Tbsp and set aside for later (for the mayonnaise!). Add the cocoa powder to the main mixture and whisk again.

3 / Line a baking sheet with baking paper. Remove any hard outer crusts from the cooled chocolate cake, then crumble it into a large bowl. Add the buttercream and stir until all the crumbs are coated and you can shape the mixture into a ball.

4 / Shape the cake mix into 12 drumstick shapes, round at one end and tapered at the other. Push a cake pop stick into the tapered end and place on the lined sheet. Freeze for 30 minutes, or until firm.

5 / Meanwhile, make the caramel ketchup following the instructions on page 67 for the red salted caramel drip. Place in a bowl, cover with plastic wrap and leave to cool in the fridge until firm.

6 / Next, make the shortbread chips. Line a baking sheet with baking paper. Cream the butter and sugar together in a stand mixer fitted with the balloon whisk attachment (or use a handheld electric whisk) until smooth and spreadable. Add the vanilla, orange zest and flour and use a spatula to roughly combine. Use your hands to form the dough into a ball. Lightly flour the work surface and place the shortbread on top. Lightly flour the top of the shortbread then use your hands to press it out. It doesn't matter if it's a bit bumpy as this will give the chips natural variation. Use a knife to cut the shortbread into chip shapes; imperfections help them look more real!

7 / Transfer the chips to the lined baking sheet and chill in the fridge for 30 minutes. Preheat the oven to 180°C [350°F/Gas mark 4].

8 / Meanwhile, put the cornflakes in a clear bag and crush using your fingers into different-sized crumbs.

9 / Once the shortbread is chilled, sprinkle the top with granulated sugar, then bake for 15–20 minutes until lightly browned. Leave to cool for 10 minutes on the sheet. Transfer to a wire rack to finish cooling.

10 / Place the white chocolate in a microweavable bowl and microwave in 15-second bursts, stirring well after each burst until fully melted. Be careful not to overheat. (If using candy melts, microwave in 30-second bursts to start with then 15-second bursts until melted.) Stir well after heating to give time for the chocolate to melt. Add the oil-based yellow food dye (must not contain water as this will cause the chocolate to seize) and stir to distribute the colour.

11 / Coat the cake pops in a thin layer of the melted chocolate (use a spoon to spread it all over), then immediately coat in the crushed cornflakes so that it covers the chocolate. Place back on the sheet and freeze for 30 minutes. Once cold, remove the stick.

12 / To serve, put the caramel ketchup and the reserved buttercream for the mayonnaise in serving bowls. Arrange the chips, putting some in a paper bag, and sprinkling with more granulated sugar. Arrange the chicken to complete the meal.

Tip: If you have time, you can make crème pât for the mayo (page 15) instead of buttercream. It will make a lot more than you need, but you can always find a good use for it!

STEP 11 ▼

New Year's Eve: Owl Cake

An owl cake for the New Year, because they represent wisdom, change and transformation. This cake hopefully won't get your feathers ruffled, it's just about getting the buttercream stroke technique right. You can always start on the back of the cake and get in the flow, before moving on to the front of the cake. Make a little wish to yourself when you pop the clock on the top of the owl's head.

"When you bake, what's most important is to have a hoot!"

SERVES: 25–30

1 quantity of Vanilla Cake (page 10) or Vegan Vanilla Cake (page 23)
1 quantity of Italian Meringue Buttercream (page 32) or American Buttercream (page 31)
black, pink, purple and orange gel food dyes
white, pink, black and orange fondant (about 65g [2¼oz] white, 70g [2½oz] pink, 8g [¼oz] black and 60g [2oz] orange)

1 homemade or store-bought round cookie (such as Rich Tea), for the clock
jam
¼ quantity of Royal Icing, dyed black (page 94)
edible glitter
gold sprinkles

Can be made vegan!

Note: Follow the instructions on page 10 or 23 depending on which vanilla cake you have chosen, but divide your cake batter between 3 x 18-cm [7-in] tins, and 2 x 15-cm [6-in] cake tins. I've given quantities and equivalent baking times below, although these are approximate! Use your eye as a guide – there is a little less than a third of the total batter in the smaller cake tins for the top tiers. The smaller tins will bake faster so just check on them and take them out earlier if necessary.

Vanilla cake
about 550g [1lb 3oz] x 3 (18-cm [7-in] cake tins) for base – bake for 30–35 minutes
about 375g [13oz] x 2 (15-cm [6-in] cake tins) for upper – bake for 25–30 minutes

Vegan vanilla cake
about 480g [17oz] x 3 (18-cm [7-in] cake tins) – bake for 25–30 minutes
about 320g [11¼oz] x 2 (15-cm [6-in] cake tins) – bake for 20–25 minutes

Tip: The Italian Meringue Buttercream is ideal for this cake as it's easiest to smooth using the palette knife, although American will work too.

1 / Make sure the cakes are cool before assembling. Stack all 5 of the layers with the smaller layers on top (there's no need for cake boards in between). Carve the 2 smaller layers so that the top is curved (it may help to chill your cake in the freezer first so that it's less fragile when carving). Crumb-coat the cakes (see page 28) using your chosen buttercream. It's fine if this is a bit rough as it will be covered by the next layer of buttercream. You should have plenty of buttercream left for the decoration. Chill the cake in the fridge until firm.

2 / Meanwhile, divide the remaining buttercream between 3 bowls and colour each using gel food dye as follows: pink, purple and orange. Place each different colour into a different piping [pastry] bag, and cut a large tip (or use a large round piping tip).

3 / For the clock, roll out 30g [1oz] of white fondant to cover your round cookie, sticking it down with jam, then pipe the clock face on using black Royal Icing.

4 / Starting from the base of the chilled cake, pipe a round blob of pink buttercream, then use a palette knife to smooth it upwards. Pipe another blob next to

it and repeat. Keep doing this until you have created a row of 5, then continue in the row above with 4 blobs, then 3 above until you have 5 decreasing rows for the owl's belly. Use this same technique to cover the whole cake – orange around the rest of the body and purple around the head.

5 / Roll out the pink fondant (use icing sugar or a tiny bit of oil to stop it sticking) and use an 8-cm [3¼-in] decorative circle cutter to stamp out 2 large circles. Roll out the remaining white fondant in the same way and cut out a 5-cm [2-in] circle. Apply the white circle on top of the pink with a little water, then place this onto the cake for eyes. Add a small black fondant circle (about 2cm [¾in] in diameter) for pupils, then decorate with glitter and gold sprinkles. You can wet the fondant with a tiny amount of water to help the glitter stick, and use a dot of icing leftover from earlier to stick on the sprinkles. Pipe the beak using orange buttercream and create a more pointed shape using an offset spatula. Pipe the ears in the same way using purple buttercream. Shape the claws from orange fondant (or you can use marzipan or the rest of the orange buttercream), then cover in edible glitter using a little water to help it stick. Finally, place the clock between the ears!

STEP 4 ▼

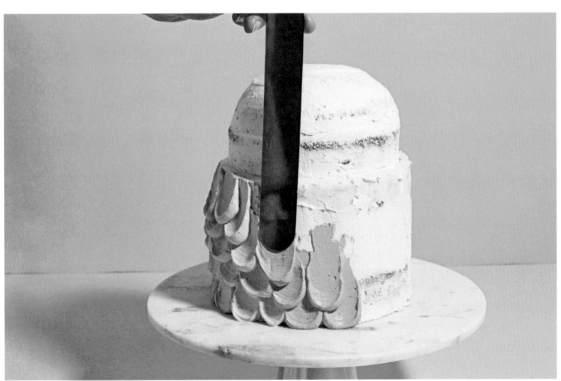

New Baby: Duck Pond

This is a fun twist on a pavlova, and a little bit different to the ordinary new baby or baby shower-style cakes! If you can make a pavlova, you can definitely make this decorated version. Even if you haven't made meringue or pavlova before, it's pretty straightforward. Just make sure you are patient when whisking the egg whites. You can't go wrong with mallowy meringue, whipped cream and fruit!

SERVES: 10–12 (MAKES: 1 SHARING-SIZED PAVLOVA)

MERINGUE
4 egg whites (about 120g [4oz])
225g [1 cup plus 2 Tbsp] caster or granulated sugar
1 Tbsp vanilla bean paste
1 Tbsp cornflour [cornstarch]
yellow gel food dye

BLUEBERRY COULIS
100g [¾ cup plus 1 tsp] fresh blueberries
35g [2½ Tbsp] caster or granulated sugar
squeeze of lemon juice

CREAM FILLING
200ml [¾ cup plus 2 Tbsp] double [heavy] cream
30g [3½ Tbsp] icing [confectioners'] sugar
1 Tbsp vanilla bean paste
blue gel food dye

PLUS
200g [1⅔ cups] fresh blueberries, strawberries
edible black pen
3 Tbsp icing [confectioners'] sugar
orange gel food dye
black food dye mixed with a small amount of vodka or alcohol-based extract

1 / Preheat the oven to 120°C [248°F/Gas mark ½]. Line a baking sheet with baking paper.

2 / For the meringue, put the egg whites into a clean, dry stand mixer fitted with the balloon whisk attachment (or use a handheld electric whisk) and whisk on high speed until stiff peaks form. Add the sugar, 1 Tbsp at a time, whisking for 30–60 seconds between each addition. When all the sugar is incorporated and the meringue is glossy with firm peaks, transfer a sixth to another bowl and set aside.

3 / Add the vanilla and cornflour to the main meringue mix and whisk until incorporated. Spoon onto the baking paper and spread into an 18–20-cm [7–8-in] circle. Use a spoon to make ridges on the side.

4 / Transfer two-thirds of the reserved meringue to a piping [pastry] bag and pipe clouds on top of a cocktail stick [toothpick]: 3 blobs in a row, then 2 above; use a finger dipped in water to flatten the tips. Add yellow food dye to the remaining meringue and use to pipe ducks: 1 blob for the body with a little flick up for the tail, then a small blob for the head. Bake everything for 1 hour 10 minutes.

5 / Meanwhile, make the blueberry coulis. Put the ingredients in a pan and simmer for 10 minutes, or until the sugar has dissolved. Leave to cool. Transfer to a blender and blend until smooth. Set aside.

6 / When the pavlova has finished baking, turn the oven off and leave the pavlova to cool in the oven with the door closed for 1–2 hours.

7 / For the cream filling, put the ingredients into a bowl with blue food dye to colour. Whip to soft peaks.

8 / Spoon a layer of fresh blueberries into the pavlova, then spoon the cream filling on top. Swirl the coulis through the cream and allow some drips down the side. Decorate with blueberries and strawberries, ducks and clouds. Use an edible black pen to mark the ducks' eyes. Mix the 3 Tbsp icing sugar with a few drops of water, a drop at a time, in a bowl to make a paste, then dye orange and pipe a little onto the duck for their beaks. You can also mix a little black food dye with a small amount of vodka and add faces to the strawberries. Put the leftover coulis in a bowl and serve alongside the pavlova.

Pride: Mirror Glaze Cake

This rainbow cheesecake celebrates Pride festival, but has an extra mirror glaze twist to elevate it to another level. If you don't want to do the mirror glaze (it can be a little bit technical!), you can always serve this without, as the layered cheesecake speaks for itself!

SERVES: 8

BASE
200g [7oz] digestive biscuits [graham crackers] (or your favourite cookie)
80g [⅓ cup] salted butter

CHEESECAKE
170ml [¾ cup minus 2 tsp] cold water
22g [2⅓ Tbsp] gelatine powder
630g [2¾ cups plus 2 tsp] cream cheese
280g [1¼ cups] mascarpone
265g [1¾ cups plus 4 tsp] icing [confectioners'] sugar
grated zest of 2 oranges
1 tsp vanilla bean paste
1¾ tsp almond extract
400ml [1⅔ cups] double [heavy] cream
red, yellow, blue, green and purple gel food dyes

MIRROR GLAZE
225g [1⅔ cups] white chocolate, finely chopped
90ml [6 Tbsp] cold water
15g [1⅔ Tbsp] gelatine powder
110ml [½ cup minus 2 tsp] water
255g [1 cup plus 1 tsp] caster or granulated sugar
180ml [¾ cup] liquid glucose
150g [⅔ cup] sweetened condensed milk
white, red, yellow, blue and green purple gel food dyes

PLUS
fondant to shape a paintbrush (push a skewer into the fondant to make it easier to stand up on the cheesecake), or use a real paintbrush if short on time

1 / First, set an entremet ring to 18-cm [7-in] diameter. Place a thin cake board or similar at the base, just slightly smaller than the tin, then line the inside of the entremet tin with food-grade acetate, using a peg or tape to secure the ends.

2 / Next, make the base. Either process the cookies in a food processor until fine, or place in a clear plastic bag and bash with a rolling pin or similar until you have mostly fine crumbs. Melt the butter, then stir into the cookie crumbs. Press into the base of the prepared acetate/ring and chill in the freezer.

3 / For the cheesecake, in a small microwaveable bowl, add the cold water then sprinkle over the gelatine powder and stir to moisten. Set aside for 5 minutes just to soften. Now microwave for around 30 seconds, or until the gelatine is dissolved. Let cool.

4 / Whisk together the cream cheese, mascarpone, icing sugar, orange zest, vanilla bean paste and almond extract until smooth, scraping down the bowl to ensure everything is mixed well. Add the cream and mix on low speed until incorporated, then whisk on high speed until thickened and fluffy.

5 / Return to the gelatine – it should be cooled but still liquid, but if it has started to set, just warm in the microwave in 5-second bursts until just melted again. Add it to the cheesecake mixture, then beat on high speed until combined.

6 / Divide the mix equally between 5 bowls. Add food dye to dye the bowls in rainbow colours.

7 / Pour the purple layer on top of the cookie base, then chill in the fridge for 30 minutes, or until semi-set. Repeat with all the different layer colours. Once all the layers have been added, place in the fridge to chill for at least 4 hours, or preferably overnight. Once chilled, you can remove the entremet ring and peel off the acetate.

8 / Next, make the mirror glaze. Add your finely chopped white chocolate to a heatproof bowl. Add the 90ml [6 Tbsp] cold water to a separate bowl and sprinkle over the gelatine. Stir to combine, then set aside for now. Add the 110ml [½ cup minus 2 tsp] water, sugar and liquid glucose to a pan, then heat over a high heat until it boils and reaches 103°C [217°F] on a sugar thermometer. Remove from the heat and whisk in the gelatine. Add the condensed milk and whisk again. Pour this over the white chocolate, then stir until it is melted and smooth. Add white food dye to colour and leave to cool to around 35°C [95°F], stirring occasionally to prevent a skin forming. Add 2 Tbsp of the mixture to 5 different bowls. Add food dye to colour each bowl as follows: red, yellow, green, blue and purple. Leave to cool to the right temperature before glazing (see below).

9 / To glaze the cheesecake, place it on a raised pedestal (any kind of bowl or ramekin that is slightly smaller than the diameter of the cheesecake) and place this on top of plastic wrap to make cleaning up easier later. When the white glaze has reached 29°C [84°F], pour it over the top. The smaller bowls of colour may cool quicker so you may need to

microwave them for a couple of seconds to warm them. Keep pouring the white glaze over until all the sides are covered. Add spoonfuls of the coloured glazes (this will be messy but that's fine!), then use a palette knife to smooth the top in 1–2 strokes. Leave to set for 30 minutes.

10 / Transfer to a serving plate and insert a fondant or real paintbrush on top (use leftover mirror glaze to add the same colours to the tips of the brush). You should be able to just pick up the plastic wrap to clean up. If you want to, you can scrape the dripped-off glaze back into a bowl to be reheated and mixed again when you want to reuse it.

Note: The photo for this is done without the drips being collected, and it's done at a slightly higher temperature so that the glaze looks semi-translucent. You could do it this way if you wanted to pour the glaze in front of your guests to wow them! Just make sure there is another plate to collect all the drips!

Tip: If you are worried about making the mirror glaze or don't have time, you can buy ready-to-use mirror glazes instead! Just follow the packet instructions.

Lunar New Year: Pineapple Cookies

Pineapple tarts are popularly eaten in the lead up to the Lunar New Year. If you are unfamiliar with these delectable bite-sized treats, the sugars in the pineapple paste filling become rich and caramelized – very different to how an ordinary pineapple would taste! This is then encased in the buttery pastry, and can be decorated as any of the 12 animal signs of the Lunar New Year, or a cute mandarin orange, which signifies wealth and luck. Alternatively, you can keep these plain and enjoy without decorating!

MAKES: AROUND 28 BITE-SIZED COOKIES

PASTRY
95g [½ cup minus 4 tsp] salted butter (or use vegan butter that is at least 75% fat content)
190g [1½ cups minus 1 Tbsp] plain [all-purpose] flour (or 190g [1½ cups minus 1 Tbsp] gluten-free flour plus 1 tsp xanthan gum)
50g [¼ cup] caster or granulated sugar
1 tsp baking powder
4–5 Tbsp cold water

PINEAPPLE FILLING
2 x 432-g [15¼-oz] cans pineapple (incuding juice)
3 Tbsp caster or granulated sugar

Can be made vegan!

1 / For the pastry, rub the butter into the flour until it resembles breadcrumbs. Stir through the sugar and baking powder, then very gradually add enough water to form a smooth but not sticky dough.

2 / For the pineapple filling, add the pineapple and its juice to a food processor and blend until as smooth as possible. Pour into a saucepan and stir occasionally over a medium-high heat until all the juice has evaporated. Add the sugar and reduce the heat to medium, stirring frequently and keeping watch to ensure the bottom does not burn. Keep stirring until it turns a deeper golden. Transfer to a bowl, cover and chill in the fridge for at least 3 hours.

3 / To shape and bake, preheat the oven to 170°C [340°F/Gas mark 3]. Divide the pineapple paste into 8-g [¼-oz] pieces, then shape these into smooth balls using the palms of your hands. Divide your pastry into 11–12-g [⅓oz] balls, pressing them into a thin circle using your fingers. You will need to colour (using gel food dye) and shape your pastry depending on which animal year it is (see overleaf).

4 / For all the designs on the following page, you will need to place the ball of pineapple paste on top of the thin circle of pastry, then bring all the sides together and press to seal into a ball. Turn over and decorate. Some of the animal shapes are a different shape to round, so for these, press the pastry into a shape that corresponds (e.g. for the snake, press the pastry into a long oblong that tapers at one end). The additional decorations on top should adhere with a little pressure, but you can use a very small dab of water to help if you need. Bake for 15–20 minutes.

RAT

You will need: Extra coloured dough – pink, plus black sesame seeds

To decorate: Create a slightly tapered oblong shape so that the face area is narrower. Use pink dough for the ears, tail and nose. Add sesame seed eyes.

OX

You will need: Extra coloured dough – brown and pink, plus blanched almonds, cut into thin slices or pine nuts (or any similar nut)

To decorate: Add a pink muzzle, then use a cocktail stick [toothpick] to create holes. Add brown patches, then bake. After baking, paint on the face and poke in the almond slices or pine nuts.

TIGER

You will need: Extra coloured dough – orange, plus black sesame seeds and orange gel food dye

To decorate: Add orange ears and nose, then add sesame seed eyes. Paint orange stripes using orange gel food dye mixed with a little water.

RABBIT

You will need: Extra coloured dough – pink, plus black sesame seeds

To decorate: Create a slightly more flattened oblong shape for the rabbit, add white ears, then add pink dough to the centres. Add pink dough for the nose, then add sesame seed eyes.

DRAGON

You will need: Extra coloured dough – red and green, plus gold (flat and round) sprinkles, edible gold paint and black sesame seeds

To decorate: Create a tapered long shape for the dragon and add coloured dough for ears and nose. Add sesame seed eyes, then add sprinkles down the back. After baking, paint areas with gold paint.

SNAKE

You will need: Extra coloured dough – red, plus black sesame seeds and red and green gel food dye

To decorate: Create a tapered oblong shape, then coil like a snake. Add sesame seed eyes, then use red dough to create a tongue. Paint a snake pattern with red and green food dye mixed with a little water.

HORSE

You will need: Extra coloured dough – brown and black

To decorate: Encase the pineapple paste with brown pastry instead of white and create a flattened oblong shape – slightly narrower at one end. Add sesame seed eyes and use white dough for the stripe down the face. Add black dough for nostrils and eyes, then add a dot of white dough to the eyes. Use more brown dough for the ears and hair.

SHEEP

You will need: Extra coloured dough – black, plus black sesame seeds

To decorate: Add sesame seed eyes. Attach 2 white balls of dough to the top, then indent the middle of each with a knife. Add black dough to either side.

MONKEY

You will need: Extra coloured dough – brown and black, plus black sesame seeds

To decorate: Use brown dough for the ears and mouth/nose area. Add white dough to the ears and to create the eye area. Add sesame seed eyes and add black and white dough for the nose and mouth.

ROOSTER

You will need: Extra coloured dough – yellow and red, plus black sesame seeds, orange star-shaped sprinkles and red heart-shaped sprinkles

To decorate: Add red sprinkles to the top of the head, then add sesame seed eyes. Create a beak and wattle with red and yellow dough, then press in star sprinkles for feet – make sure to push them in properly so they don't pop out again during baking.

DOG

You will need: Extra coloured dough – brown and black, plus black sesame seeds

To decorate: Add sesame seed eyes, then use brown dough to create ears and nose area. Add black dough for the nose.

PIG

You will need: Extra coloured dough – pink, plus black sesame seeds

To decorate: Use pink dough to create the ears and snout, then use a cocktail stick [toothpick] to create holes and add sesame seed eyes.

ORANGE

You will need: Orange and green dough, plus black sesame seeds

To decorate: Shape using the orange dough, then add green dough for the leaves. Add sesame seed eyes, then use a cocktail stick to indent a smile and create a dimpled effect.

Bonfire Night: Phoenix Cake

This is a fiery phoenix cake to celebrate British Bonfire Night in a slightly fantastical way. Make the spring roll wrapper sail decorations the night before and enjoy the decorating process the next day!

SERVES: 20–25

RICE PAPER SPRING ROLL WRAPPER SAILS
about 8–10 rice paper spring roll wrappers
red, yellow and orange gel food dyes
edible gold paint

PLUS
choose a cake recipe (see pages 10–26), baked and cooled – the Crème Brûlée Cake (page 15) will work perfectly as the caramelized sugar

top works well with this design, although you can always use a different cake, and still brûlée the top!
1 quantity of American Buttercream (page 31) or Italian Meringue Buttercream (page 32)
red fondant
edible gold leaf
3 Tbsp caster or granulated sugar, for the top

"Flame as high as you can!"

Can be made vegan!

1 / Make the red rice paper spring roll wrapper sails following the instructions on page 30 and leave to dry overnight. Once dry, you can paint some of the edges and folds with a little edible gold paint.

2 / Make sure the cakes are cool before assembling. Stack and crumb-coat the cakes (see pages 27–28) using your chosen buttercream. Reserve plenty of buttercream for decoration. Chill the cake in the fridge until firm.

3 / Meanwhile, shape a baby phoenix using red fondant, adding edible gold leaf and painting with food dye to add interest.

4 / Spread a second coat of buttercream all over the chilled crumb coat using a palette knife and smooth again. Leave the top edge rough, then paint the rim gold. Chill in the fridge until firm again.

5 / While the cake is chilling, divide the remaining buttercream between 3 bowls and colour yellow, orange and red using food dye. Once the base has chilled, use a palette knife to paint strokes of the coloured buttercream to look like a flame. Apply gold leaf for added interest.

6 / Sprinkle the sugar over the (chilled) buttercream on top of the cake, then using a handheld blowtorch, caramelize the sugar. Place the phoenix on top and arrange smaller sails to look like its wings. Stick more sails into the side of the cake, arranging them so that it looks like they are all part of one tall flame.

Tip: Use around 5–6 rice paper sails for up the sides of the cake and on top, then 2 for the wings and another for the tail. The wings are slightly smaller! I recommend making more sails than needed, then picking the ones that fit best when decorating the cake. Vary the sizes to make it interesting.

Thanksgiving: Turkeys

These are made using a German cookie dough which is extremely delicate and has a melt in-the-mouth texture thanks to the addition of potato starch. You can replace the potato starch with plain flour if liked, but this will result in a more ordinary shortbread. Feel free to experiment with your family of turkeys!

Can be made vegan!

MAKES: ABOUT 12, DEPENDING ON SIZE OF TURKEYS

250g [1 cup plus 2 Tbsp] salted butter, at room temperature, cubed (or use with vegan butter, at least 75% fat content)

80g [½ cup plus 1 Tbsp] icing [confectioners'] sugar
1 tsp vanilla bean paste
250g [1⅓ cups] potato starch

160g [1¼ cups] plain [all-purpose] flour (or use gluten-free flour plus 1½ tsp xanthan gum), plus extra for dusting

black, yellow, orange, red and brown gel food dyes

PLUS
¼ quantity of Royal Icing (page 94)

1 / Line a baking sheet with baking paper. Place the butter cubes and icing sugar in a stand mixer (or use a handheld electric whisk) fitted with the balloon whisk attachment and cream together until light and fluffy. Add the vanilla bean paste and mix again until combined. Sift in the potato starch and flour, then use a spatula to mix into a paste. Avoid overmixing. Combine into a ball using your hands.

2 / Divide the dough into different portions, reserve about a third for the brown turkey bodies and then a small ball for the eyes (white and black dough). Divide the remaining dough so that the orange dough will be about twice as much as the red, and the yellow dough will be about twice as much as the orange. Colour each portion by kneading in the gel food dye. Try to handle the dough lightly and as little as possible. This will help to stop the dough sticking to your hands, plus the less you handle it, the more the cookies will crumble and melt in your mouth.

3 / On a floured surface, roll out the yellow, orange and red dough, then use round cutters to stamp out a circle from each – with the red dough being the smallest and the yellow being the largest. Stick the orange dough onto the yellow, and the red onto the orange (using a little water to help it stick). Use the large circle cutter just to cut into the base a little more so that it's less rounded. Use tools to press dots

on the dough. These are the turkeys' feathers. Place on the lined baking sheet.

Note: I use 8.25-cm [3¼-in], 6.25-cm [2½-in] and 4.5-cm [1¾-in] cutters, but as long as you have 3 different-sized circular cutters it will work fine.

4 / Next, make the turkeys' bodies. Stick a smaller ball of brown dough on top of a larger ball, squishing down so that they are flattened a little. Add the nose/beak using leftover yellow dough. Add the eyes using the black and white dough. Add the feet by cutting a star shape from the orange dough and sticking on. Repeat and make lots of turkeys of all shapes and sizes. You can add eyebrows, flowers, necklaces, ties, etc. to all the roosters to personalize them. Lie the bodies on their backs on the lined baking sheet. Chill for 15–30 minutes in the fridge. Preheat the oven to 160°C [325°F/Gas mark 3].

5 / Put the baking sheet in the oven and bake the feathers for about 12 minutes. If they're ready you should be able to easily slide a palette knife underneath and transfer to a wire rack. Just be careful not to drop them as they're very fragile. Leave the bodies to bake for 20 minutes in total. They will expand a little and may crack very slightly, but will hold their shape well. Transfer to a wire rack and leave to cool. Once cool, use a little Royal Icing to stick the turkeys to their feathers.

Mid-Autumn Festival: Snowskin Mooncakes

Mooncakes are traditionally eaten during the Mid-Autumn Festival. The traditional version you will see the most has a stamped golden brown pastry exterior, with a red bean or lotus paste filling, and sometimes a duck egg yolk. The pastry uses lye water (which can be dangerous if not used correctly), so this version is a modern twist using a mochi wrapper instead! This is a fun way to create lots of different colours and tastes amazing (particularly if you enjoy mochi), plus the custard filling is loved by everyone!

MAKES: AROUND 12

THICK CUSTARD FILLING
2 medium egg yolks (replace with extra 2 Tbsp cornflour [cornstarch] plus 4 Tbsp plant-based milk to make vegan)
30g [2½ Tbsp] caster or granulated sugar
25g [¼ cup] cornflour [cornstarch], plus extra for dusting
130ml [½ cup plus 2 tsp] milk or plant-based milk
1 Tbsp vanilla bean paste

25g [1⅔ Tbsp] butter or vegan butter

SNOWSKIN WRAPPERS
60g [½ cup minus 2 tsp] glutinous rice flour, plus extra for dusting
70g [½ cup] rice flour
40g [½ cup minus 2 tsp] cornflour [cornstarch]
30g [3½ Tbsp] icing [confectioners'] sugar
240ml [1 cup plus 1 Tbsp] milk or plant-based milk
2 Tbsp vegetable oil

2 Tbsp condensed milk or vegan coconut condensed milk (this makes it creamier, though you could just substitute whole milk or plant-based milk if you don't have condensed milk to hand!)

PLUS
green, pink and yellow gel food dyes

Naturally gluten free!

Can be made vegan!

1 / First, make the thick custard filling. Whisk the eggs yolks (or vegan replacement), sugar and cornflour together in a heatproof bowl. Add the milk and vanilla bean paste to a small pan, then heat over a medium heat until just starting to bubble. Pour a small amount over the egg yolk mixture, whisking quickly and constantly as you pour. Gradually add the rest of the milk, still continuing to whisk constantly. When it is all mixed together, pour back into the pan and return to the heat.

2 / Continue whisking until the mixture is very, very stiff (can hold a spoon upright in it). Remove from the heat and add the butter, then stir until it melts in. Transfer to a bowl, cover with plastic wrap and chill in the fridge until firm.

Tip: When the custard mixture thickens and starts looking like it might go lumpy just take it off the stove temporarily and whisk again until smooth before returning to the heat. You need short bursts of heat, but you will need to take it off the stove to catch up with whisking, as this custard gets very thick!

3 / When chilled, line a plate with baking paper. Shape the custard into 12 x 30-g [1-oz] round balls. Flour your hands and the work surface lightly to prevent sticking while shaping. Place these on the lined plate and leave in the fridge for now.

4 / For the snowskin wrappers, add all the ingredients to a microwaveable bowl and whisk together until smooth and combined. Cover with plastic wrap and microwave on high in 1-minute bursts, whisking well after each burst. You will need to microwave it for a total of 3–4 minutes, and switch to mixing with a spatula towards the end as it will get very thick.

5 / Once the mixture is thick, turn it out onto a surface coated with a generous amount of glutinous rice flour (or cornflour) to prevent sticking. Divide into 12 x 30-g [1-oz] individual pieces. Use your fingers to press a piece into a rough circle shape (slightly thicker in the middle than the sides), making sure to use enough glutinous rice flour/cornflour to prevent sticking. Place a ball of custard in the centre and lift the sides of the dough up to encase the filling, pressing together firmly on top to seal. Turn this around so the base is now the top.

6 / Use a 50-g [1¾-oz] mooncake plunger to mould the mooncakes. This is much easier than it looks! Just brush the mould with a little glutinous rice flour (or cornflour), then place the mould on top of the mooncake and push down on the plunger, holding for a few seconds to ensure a good print. Lift up and remove your shaped mooncake!

Tip: You can make these different colours by dividing the snowskin wrapper dough into different bowls and mixing in gel food dye. You can also create marbled effects by combining 2 or 3 colours. You can also make larger mooncakes, just always use similar proportions of wrapper to filling.

Easter: Hot Cross Bunnies

These will make your house smell wonderful, and you can have fun creating whatever bunny shapes you like out of the non-yeasted dough! The dough is quite wet and sticky, particularly before its first rise, so a stand mixer or bread machine is recommended to make these – although you can work by hand if you're confident with wet dough and a dough scraper. The bunnies are more for decoration rather than eating!

MAKES: 16

DOUGH

200ml [¾ cup plus 2 Tbsp] whole milk
1 cinnamon stick
3 cardamon pods
1 small star anise
500g [3½ cups] strong white flour, plus extra for dusting
60g [5 Tbsp] caster or granulated sugar
2 tsp ground cinnamon
1 tsp ground ginger
¼ tsp grated nutmeg
pinch of cloves
grated zest of 1 orange and 1 lemon
7g [2¼ tsp] fast-action dried [active dry] yeast
1 tsp salt
100ml [⅓ cup plus 1 Tbsp] water
2 eggs
65g [¼ cup plus 1 tsp] unsalted butter, softened at room temperature
180g [1¼ cups 1 tsp] mixed dried fruit and peel
sunflower or other neutral-tasting oil, for oiling

BUNNIES

150g [1 cup plus 2 Tbsp] plain [all-purpose] flour
pinch of salt
85ml [⅓ cup] water
black, pink and orange gel food dye to add details

CROSS

50g [6 Tbsp] plain [all-purpose] flour
55ml [¼ cup] water

PLUS

beaten egg, to glaze
apricot jam to glaze

1 / For the dough, pour the milk into a pan and add the whole spices. Bring to a simmer, then remove from the heat and let cool and infuse for 20 minutes.

2 / Add the flour, sugar, ground spices, grated citrus zest, yeast and salt to a large bowl and stir together. Add the water to the tepid milk, then add the eggs and whisk together. Pour the liquid over the dry ingredients. With the dough hook attachment and the stand mixer on low, let the machine knead the dough for 8 minutes. Add the softened butter and let the machine knead it in until fully incorporated.

3 / Put in a bowl, cover with plastic wrap and rise at room temperature for 1½–3 hours until doubled in size.

Note: This dough is enriched with butter, milk and eggs, so rises a lot slower than other doughs! If it doesn't look any bigger after an hour or so, don't worry, it will rise; just give it more time.

4 / When risen, roll out the dough on a generously floured work surface, scatter the mixed dried fruit over, then roll up and knead until the fruit is evenly distributed. Divide into 16 pieces and shape into smooth circles. Arrange in an oiled 26-cm [10½-in] square tin. Loosely cover with oiled plastic wrap and leave to prove for 1–2 hours at room temperature, or in the fridge until doubled in size.

5 / Meanwhile, make the bunnies by mixing together the flour, salt and water. Roll a ball of dough for the body, then roll a smaller ball for the head and stick it on top. Shape ears using your fingers, then attach to the bunny's head (you may need to squeeze a bit to ensure the ear attaches), then use your fingers to adjust the shape of the ears again. Add legs using more dough. Use the remaining dough to shape into carrots. Paint the bunny's face and ears using black and pink food dye diluted with a tiny bit of water and the carrots using orange food dye.

6 / When the buns have doubled in size, preheat the oven to 200°C [400°F/Gas mark 6]. Brush the beaten egg over the buns to glaze. Mix the flour and water together in a small bowl to make the paste for the cross, then place in a piping [pastry] bag, cut a tip and pipe crosses over each bun. Nestle the bunnies into the dough.

7 / Bake for 10 minutes, then reduce the oven to 180°C [350°F/Gas mark 4] and bake for a further 15 minutes, or until golden brown. As soon as they are out of the oven, glaze with apricot jam and leave to cool in the tin for 10 minutes before transferring to a wire rack to finish cooling.

STEP 5 ▼

STEP 6 ▼

Easter: Rum Baabaa...

The name of this classic French dessert – the 'rum baba' – perfectly suits becoming an Easter treat featuring sheep. Ideally, you do need a stand mixer or bread machine for this dough, as it is very wet and more like a pipeable batter consistency! You can also beat it by hand with a spatula, but it will just take longer to develop the gluten (and it will really work your arm muscles!). Choose to decorate yours with just cream and marzipan, or add the white marshmallows – and as long as ewe follow the instructions carefully, it'll all go wool!

MAKES: 18–24

DOUGH
265g [1¾ cups plus 4 tsp] strong white flour
1 tsp salt
5g [1⅔ tsp] fast-action dried [active-dry] yeast
40g [3¼ Tbsp] caster or granulated sugar
80ml [⅓ cup] whole milk
4 medium eggs
100g [⅓ cup plus 1 Tbsp] unsalted butter, very soft and spreadable, plus extra for greasing

RUM SOAKING SYRUP
120g [⅔ cup] caster or granulated sugar
500ml [2 cups plus 2 Tbsp] water
finely grated zest of 1 orange
120ml [½ cup] rum

PLUS
800ml [3⅓ cups] double [heavy] cream
150g [½ cup] marzipan (page 121) or use storebought
75g [½ cup plus ½ Tbsp] icing [confectioners'] sugar
blue and black gel food dye
pretzel sticks, or similar
mini white marshmallows (optional)

1 / For the dough, add the flour, salt, yeast and sugar to a stand mixer bowl. Warm the milk in the microwave until tepid, then add to the bowl along with the eggs. Add the soft butter in chunks, then beat on a slow speed (with the paddle attachment) until the mixture is very smooth and elastic.

2 / Cover the dough with oiled plastic wrap and leave to rise for 2–3 hours at room temperature until doubled in size. The rising time varies depending on the ambient temperature, and you should expect this dough to take longer to rise than a dough that isn't enriched with milk, eggs and butter.

3 / When risen, use a spatula to transfer the dough to a large piping [pastry] bag. Cut a medium tip, then

pipe into greased 6-cup doughnut tins or individual 7-cm [2¾-in] savarin moulds. They should be about half full.

4 / Lightly cover with oiled plastic wrap and leave to prove for 1–2 hours at room temperature until doubled in size; the dough should be reaching the tops of the moulds. This second rise will be quicker than the first, so keep an eye out.

5 / Preheat the oven to 180°C [350°F/Gas mark 4] and bake for 10–12 minutes. The baabaas should be golden on top.

6 / While they bake, prepare the rum soaking syrup. Place the sugar, water and orange zest in a large

pan and bring to the boil, stirring intermittently, Once all the sugar has dissolved and the mixture has come to the boil, reduce to a simmer and add the rum. Simmer for a minute, then remove from the heat.

7 / When the baabaas have finished baking, slide them out of their tins (this should be very easy) and immediately soak them in the warm rum syrup for about 15 seconds on each side. Use a slotted spoon to transfer them to a wire rack to drain and cool.

8 / Whip the double cream to soft peaks, then transfer a small amount to a piping bag with a 1M, 2D or similar piping tip attachment. Don't add all the cream at once, as the cream at the top will become warm from your hands, and may also end up overwhipped by the time you get to piping it out. Pipe cream in a swirl on top of each baabaa.

9 / Roll small pieces of marzipan for the sheep faces. Add little marzipan ears and position the head in the centre of the cream swirl. Make a water icing by whisking together the icing sugar with a few small drops of water. You want to create a piping consistency, so be careful not to add too much water. Divide between 2 bowls and add blue food dye to one and black to the other. Transfer both to separate small piping bags. Cut a very small tip on both, and use to pipe the facial features. Spoon or pipe (using a little cream in a small piping bag) a little blob of cream on to all the sheeps' foreheads, then poke pretzel sticks (or similar) into the rum baabaas for the sheeps' legs.

Tip: Alternatively, you can make sheep using white marshmallows – just arrange mini marshmallows all around, on top of the piped cream. If decorating this way, it's easier to place the ears after placing the marshmallows, so that they sit on top.

STEPS 8 and 9 ▼

Yuki Matsuri: Mochi Ice Cream

The process for the sugar glass here may sound daunting, but if you follow the steps carefully, you will find it's quite straightforward and quick to do once you get the hang of it. It's also incredibly impressive and a useful skill to learn! Paired with delicious mochi ice cream and tiny penguins, looking at this dessert is like stepping onto another planet. Not to mention a tasty one... perfect for celebrating Yuki Matsuri, the annual Sapporo Snow Festival.

"Every snow often, things don't go to plan. Keep ploughing through until it thaws over."

SERVES: 1 SHARING-SIZED PORTION / 10–12 MOCHI ICE-CREAM BALLS

MOCHI ICE CREAM
12 small portions of ice cream of your choice (each portion about 2 Tbsp)
160g [1 cup] glutinous rice flour, plus extra for sprinkling
65g [⅓ cup plus 1 tsp] caster or granulated sugar
220ml [1 cup minus 1 Tbsp] water
blue gel food dye

MINI FONDANT PENGUINS
white, black and orange fondant (you don't need very much, just a pinch each of black and orange fondant and 20g [¾oz] of white)

edible black pen (or black food dye, mixed with a tiny amount of water or vodka)
star-shaped yellow/orange sprinkles (for the penguin feet)

EDIBLE SUGAR GLASS BOWL
150g [¾ cup] caster or granulated sugar
100ml [⅓ cup plus 4 tsp] liquid glucose
35ml [2⅓ Tbsp] water
blue gel food dye

---

1 / First, create 12 scoops of ice cream, about 2 Tbsp each, then place on a sheet of baking paper and return to the freezer.

2 / Next, make mini penguins from fondant. Shape an oval from white fondant, then roll out some black fondant thinly and cut it to fit over the white oval with a pointed bit at the top of the head. Press to stick into place. Mould little black wings and stick to the sides. Next, attach a little nose made from orange fondant. Draw the eyes with edible black pen or black food dye mixed with a little water or vodka. Attach little star-shaped sprinkles for the feet.

3 / Next, make the mochi skin. Add the glutinous rice flour, sugar and water to a microwaveable bowl and whisk until combined. Cover and microwave on high for 1 minute. Remove from the microwave and whisk. It will still be mostly liquid at this point so won't be too difficult to mix. Cover again and heat for another 30 seconds. It will be thicker now; whisk again and return to the microwave. Keep heating in 30-second bursts and whisking or stirring after each. When the mixture becomes thick, switch to stirring with a spatula as it will just clump inside the whisk. After a total of about 4 minutes, the dough should look slightly translucent and be very sticky and thickened.

4 / Divide the mochi dough between 2 bowls; add blue food dye to one and stir in using the spatula.

5 / Sprinkle a generous amount of glutinous rice flour (or cornflour [cornstarch]) onto a work surface, then place the blue mochi dough on top. Sprinkle more glutinous rice flour on top. Roll out to about 5mm [¼in] thick while checking that it isn't sticking to your work surface (if so, use more glutinous rice flour/cornflour). Leave to cool for about 15–30 minutes.

6 / Once cool, cut out 6 circles using a 9-cm [3½-in] round cutter. Brush off the excess rice flour on top, then place a scoop of ice cream in the centre. Lift the edges of the dough to encase the ice cream, then press together at the top to seal. Work quickly to prevent the ice cream from melting! Once done, immediately wrap in plastic wrap (to help it keep its shape) and place in the freezer to firm up. Repeat to make all 6 blue mochi ice creams, then repeat with the white mochi.

7 / Next, make the edible sugar glass bowl. Fill a balloon with cold water from the tap and knot the top. Place the balloon, knot side down, in a bowl

(smaller than the balloon so that sugar doesn't drip and attach to the bowl). Make sure to have some baking paper underneath the bowl to stop sugar dripping on and sticking to your work surface.

8 / Add the sugar, liquid glucose and water to a small pan and stir to combine. Heat over a high heat. Don't stir at all until the mixture reaches 150°C [302°F]. At this point, remove the pan from the heat and stir through a couple drops of blue food dye (but don't stir through completely – leave the swirls). Leave the mixture to cool to 130–133°C [266–271°F] (it will cool quite quickly so keep an eye on it). Immediately pour over the balloon in a circular motion. Leave for about 10–15 minutes until set.

9 / Lift the balloon off the bowl and hold over the sink. Use scissors to cut a small hole in the base, as close to the knot as you can get, letting the all water drain out (try to avoid the water touching the sugar). You will then be able to gently pull the balloon away from the sugar glass.

10 / Fill your sugar glass bowl with your mochi ice-cream balls and little penguins. Serve straightaway!

STEP 6 ▼

Diwali: Nankhatai

These are traditional, popular Indian shortbread cookies, which are also enjoyed during Diwali. They are soft and full of flavour – and being eggless, are very easy to make vegan. These ones are decorated with dog designs (and some sneaky alpacas!), not only because dogs are very cute, but also because in Nepal, the second day of Diwali is all about giving dogs recognition and honour (they get adorned with garlands and flowers, and are fed well!), as in Hindu tradition the dog is a messenger and guards the gates of the afterlife.

"Great things happen when you leashed expect it."

MAKES: 14–18 (EACH 20–25G [¾–1 OZ])

125g [1 cup minus 1 Tbsp] plain [all-purpose] flour (or use 125g [1 cup minus 1 Tbsp] gluten-free flour plus ¼ tsp xanthan gum)
60g [½ cup] chickpea or besan flour
2 Tbsp fine semolina
80g [½ cup plus 1 Tbsp] icing [confectioners'] sugar

2 tsp green cardamom powder (finely ground fresh from seeds for the best flavour)
125g [½ cup plus 1 Tbsp] vegan (or dairy-based) butter (at least 75% fat content for good results), melted
1 tsp vanilla bean paste

PLUS
flaked [slivered] almonds and pecans, to decorate
1 quantity of Royal Icing (page 94)
black, blue and pink gel food dyes

Can be made vegan!

1 / Line 2 large baking sheets with baking paper. Mix the plain flour, chickpea flour, semolina, icing sugar and cardamom together in a large bowl. Add the melted butter and vanilla bean paste and mix together with a large spoon or spatula until roughly mixed together.

2 / Use your hands to press the dough together into a ball.

3 / Divide the dough into small 20–25-g [¾–1-oz] balls (you can vary the size a little bit if you like!), then roll each ball in the palms of your hands to smooth and arrange on the lined baking sheets. Press gently to flatten them.

4 / Press almonds and pecans into the dough to represent ears and nose (see photo opposite), then chill in the fridge for 30 minutes. Meanwhile, preheat the oven to 160°C [325°F/Gas mark 3].

5 / Bake the chilled cookies for 15–20 minutes (or a little longer for larger ones). They will still be soft once baked, but will firm up as they cool. Leave to cool on the baking sheet for 10 minutes before transferring to a wire rack to finish cooling.

6 / Once cool, you can decorate them. Transfer a quarter of the Royal Icing to a piping [pastry] bag. Divide the remaining icing between 3 small bowls and colour one black, one blue and the other a peach colour for the tongue. Place the colours into separate piping bags, snip a very small tip on each piping bag and use to pipe on the face details.

Diwali: Lemon, Raspberry & Rose Mandala Cheesecake

This naturally vegan cheesecake packs a lot of flavour – the freeze-dried raspberries add a very concentrated flavour without adding water, which would affect the smooth, rich creaminess of the cheesecake. It's definitely not healthy, but the cashew nuts help to make this a tasty and filling dessert/snack, while the lemon helps to keep it very refreshing. Once decorated, you can either serve it and eat it straightaway, or put the rest back in the freezer for a perfect snack any time. The cheesecake will go soft at room temperature, so it's best eaten straight from the freezer, plus the way it melts in your mouth is part of the experience. It's a bit like an ice cream! You could even make mini individual portions if you want (this is what I do)!

MAKES: 8 SLICES

CHEESECAKE
340g [2¾ cups plus 2 tsp] cashew nuts
grated zest and juice of 3 lemons
225ml [1 cup minus 1 Tbsp] coconut milk, plus 2–3 tsp extra
110g [½ cup] melted coconut oil
225g [⅔ cup] golden syrup [light corn syrup] or agave syrup

4½ tsp freeze-dried raspberry powder (ground to a fine powder in a pestle and mortar or spice grinder)
⅓ tsp rose water
pink, blue and peach gel food dyes
grated zest and juice of 1 extra lemon

COOKIE BASE
210g [7½oz] speculoos
105g [7 Tbsp] vegan butter

1 / First, for the cheesecake, soak the cashews in boiling water for 1 hour, then drain.

2 / For the cookie base, blitz the cookies in a food processor until fine, or place in a clear plastic bag and bash with a rolling pin or similar until you have mostly fine crumbs. Melt the butter, then stir into the cookie crumbs. Press into the base of an 18-cm [7-in] cake tin and chill in the freezer while you make the cheesecake filling.

3 / Drain the soaked cashews and add to a blender along with the lemon zest and blend until smooth.

4 / Add the 225ml [1 cup minus 1 Tbsp] coconut milk, lemon juice, melted coconut oil and chosen syrup and blend again until smooth.

5 / Set aside 170g [6oz] (this is for the pattern on top), then divide the remaining mixture in half. To one half, add the freeze-dried raspberry powder and rose water. Add pink food dye to give this a more

distinctive colour (although this is optional). Pour over the cookie base and chill again in the freezer for at least 1 hour until firm. To the second half, add the grated zest and juice of the extra lemon. Once the first layer is chilled/semi-set, pour the second bowl of mixture over it and chill again for another 1 hour.

6 / To create the mandala design, add a little extra coconut milk, 1 tsp at a time, to the mixture set aside earlier. You want this to flow well when you drag your cocktail stick [toothpick] through, so test this on a plate before working on the cheesecake. You can always adjust the consistency with more coconut milk after adding the food dyes.

7 / Spoon a thin layer of the thinned mixture on top of the chilled cheesecake, then divide the remaining mixture into different bowls and colour using gel food dye. You can use whatever colours you like, but having at least 3 colours looks best! Place the different colours into separate piping [pastry] bags and cut small tips on each (or use a small round piping tip). There are lots of patterns you could

create but as a starting point to begin the pattern, pipe a large dot in the centre, then pipe a smaller different coloured dot in the centre of that one. Pipe a few circles in different colours around the circumference, building outwards. Using a cocktail stick, drag from the outside of the circle to the middle, repeating at intervals all the way round the circle, and you'll see the colours start to look more like a flower. Keep building your design from there, adding dots of colour, layering them and dragging the cocktail stick through to create different effects. Experiment and see where it takes you!

8 / Chill the cheesecake for 4–6 hours in the freezer, then warm the outside of the tin with a warm cloth to help the cheesecake come out cleanly and serve. It's easier if the cheesecake is cut with a warmed knife. If it isn't all eaten then the rest can be kept in the freezer.

Tip: You can use food-grade acetate around the inside of your tin before layering up, and this will make removing the cheesecake much easier!

STEP 7 ▼

- EVERY OCCASION -

Day of the Dead: Antigravity Cake

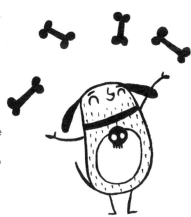

The Day of the Dead or Día de los Muertos is a Mexican celebration of life and death. The sharp demarcation between the 2 sides of this cake is representative of how the dead and living reunite over this holiday and it's full of colour just like the vibrant celebrations and *ofrendas* (collections of items that are important to or identify the person who has died).

This cake needs to be flipped to create the impressive antigravity drips, but don't worry, as long as the cake is really cold, it will flip very easily! The angled line between the black and white may also look challenging, but with a piece of baking paper covering one side, it really isn't that hard.

Can be made vegan!

SERVES: 20–25

SUGAR SKULL COOKIE
½ quantity of Ginger and Orange Cookie dough (page 94) (or you can use fondant – just leave to dry out after cutting to shape)
½ quantity of Royal Icing (page 94)
gel food dyes of choice

GANACHE DRIP
130g [¾ cup] white chocolate, finely chopped
60g [¼ cup] double [heavy] cream
pink, yellow, green and blue gel food dyes (normally this would cause chocolate to sieze, but in this case it is fine because the cream already contains a lot of water)
white food dye (optional)

VEGAN ROYAL ICING DRIP ALTERNATIVE
30–35ml [2–2⅓ Tbsp] aquafaba
170g [1¼ cups minus 1 tsp] icing [confectioners'] sugar
gel food dyes

PLUS
1 wooden skewer
choose 1 cake recipe (see pages 10–26) – the Red Velvet Cake on page 18 or the vegan version on page 26 would work very well because of the burst of colour – baked and cooled
1 quantity of American Buttercream (page 31) or Italian Meringue Buttercream (page 32)
black gel food dye
2 Tbsp cocoa powder (ideally black/heavily dutched)
colourful sprinkles

1 / For the sugar skull cookie, you will have more than enough Ginger and Orange Cookie dough, but you can use the rest for anything you want, such as some more decorated skulls, or you can just bake extra and snack on them. Make a cardboard cut-out shape of a skull, then cut around this on the cookie dough. Transfer to a lined baking sheet, then press a wooden skewer into the back of each cookie so they will bake on to this. The skewer will be inserted into the cake later so the cookie will be able to stand up. Bake and cool the cookies following the instructions on page 94, then decorate with Royal Icing (see the Kransekake on page 94 for more advice on piping). Leave the icing to set, uncovered, for at least 4 hours, or preferably overnight. Setting time depends on humidity.

2 / Divide the remaining royal icing into different bowls, colour with any food dyes you like, then place them into different piping [pastry] bags and pipe your design onto your cookie sugar skull. Set aside for now.

3 / Make sure the cakes are cool before assembling. Stack and crumb-coat the cakes on a cake board (see pages 27–28) using your chosen buttercream. Reserve plenty of buttercream for decoration. Chill the cake in the fridge until firm.

4 / Use a knife to mark a diagonal line in the buttercream on the crumb-coated cake as a guide for where you will divide your black and white buttercream. Reserve some buttercream for piping later and split the remaining buttercream between 2 bowls. Colour one black and the other white (use white food dye for a pure white look). For the black buttercream, add a few Tbsp of cocoa powder first. This will give it a dark base and make your black food dye go a lot further, otherwise you will need to use lots of black food dye to colour it. The buttercream also often darkens over time, so you may find that at first it looks like it isn't black enough, but wait an hour and it will have darkened further. Use a palette knife to spread the black buttercream on one side of the marked line. Smooth as normal – just use a knife to remove any buttercream that goes over the line. Don't worry about getting the line straight on top or smoothing a lot, as the cake will be flipped and the top will become the bottom! Place in the fridge or freezer to chill until firm.

5 / When chilled, repeat the same process with the white buttercream on the other side. Cover the black buttercream with baking paper, ensuring it lines right up to the edge. This will ensure you get a neat distinct line between the 2 colours. If any buttercream does go over by any chance (it shouldn't do as the paper really helps!), you can scrape it off with a palette knife, as the contrasting colour underneath should be set firm. Chill again.

6 – for the ganache drip / Put the white chocolate into a heatproof bowl. Pour the cream into a small saucepan and heat over a medium heat until it just starts to bubble (or heat in the microwave for about 45 seconds). Pour it over the white chocolate pieces, making sure they are fully submerged and covered, and leave to stand for 2 minutes (set a timer), then stir until all the chocolate has melted. Divide into 4 different bowls and add gel food dye to colour. Leave the mixture to cool until it is the correct consistency. You will find that the ganache drip is a pale yellow colour rather than pure white, so for a bright colour you may need to add a bit of white food dye as a base to help the colours pop.

Tip: Make sure your ganache is of a good dripping consistency, which depends on its temperature. If it's too warm it will be too thin and run too fast, but if it's too cold it will be too thick and will look blobby rather than elegant. Check for the correct consistency by practising some drips down the edge of a mug. Use a simple metal spoon to control a drip down its side. If your ganache is too warm, put it into the fridge for a minute or more (keep a close eye on it). If it's too cool, heat it in the microwave for 5–10 seconds. When you know you have the correct consistency, only then work on your actual cake (it's best to make sure it's properly chilled before you start). You can use your spoon to just gently push a few drips down the side of the cake, although for this cake using a piping [pastry] bag is better as control is essential!

6 – for the vegan royal icing drip alternative / Whisk in enough aquafaba with the icing sugar until it is a good dripping consistency (test this on the side of a glass, and if necessary adjust with more icing sugar to thicken or more aquafaba to thin). Colour and pipe on the side of the cake in the same way as the ganache. When flipping the cake, be careful not to smudge the drips, as it won't set firm like ganache.

7 / Put your different-coloured ganache drips into individual piping bags, knot to seal the tops and cut a small tip on each. Use to pipe drips just down the black half, being very careful to not let the drips pass the 50/50 line. Press sprinkles into the drips, then chill in the freezer until very firm.

8 / Next, you're going to flip the cake (sounds scary but it's very easy if your whole cake is very cold). Place a cake board or serving plate on top, then flip the whole thing. Remove the cake board on top (which previously was on the bottom). Now, cover the new top with buttercream in the same way as before, creating a line to divide the 2 colours. Carefully spread the buttercream to the edges and chill again. Do another ganache drip, this time on the white buttercream side. You may need to reheat the bag for a few seconds in the microwave (only if using a ganache drip, vegan drip will be fine!).

9 / Place a heaped spoon of buttercream in a few bowls. Add food dye to colour, then mix. Place each colour into a separate piping bag, then use to pipe swirls of colourful buttercream on top using a 1M or 2D piping tip (or other decorative piping tip). Adorn with sprinkles and top with the cookie sugar skull!

Hanami: Cherry Blossom Tree Cake

Not only does this cake have a candy floss cherry blossom tree and actual cherry blossoms within the jelly layer, but when you cut into this cake, each slice will have a cherry blossom tree pattern within it! A triple cherry blossom tree cake! The sakura extract really ties the flavour in with the design, but it can be tricky to find, so it's absolutely fine to substitute it with a different floral flavour, such as rose water or orange blossom water.

"We all blossom in our own time."

SERVES: 8 (MAKES: 1 X 18-CM [7-IN] CAKE)

CAKE
butter, for greasing
¼ quantity of the batter for the Vanilla Cake (page 10) or Vegan Vanilla Cake (page 23)
2 Tbsp unsweetened cocoa powder
35g [heaping 2 Tbsp] pink sprinkles

CHOCOLATE SHORTBREAD TREE BARK
100g [7 Tbsp] salted butter (or vegan butter, at least 75% fat content), at room temperature
45g [3 Tbsp] caster or granulated sugar
160g [1¼ cups] plain [all-purpose] flour (or use gluten-free flour plus ½ tsp xanthan gum), plus extra for dusting
10g [2 tsp] unsweetened cocoa powder

BUTTERCREAM
100g [7 Tbsp] butter (or vegan butter, at least 75% fat content)
190g [1⅓ cups] icing [confectioners'] sugar
½ tsp sakura extract (or use another floral extract such as rose water or orange blossom water, to taste)

CHERRY BLOSSOM JELLY
600ml [2½ cups] water
70g [⅓ cup] caster or granulated sugar
1⅓ tsp agar agar powder
pink food dye
5 pickled cherry blossoms

PLUS
¼ quantity of Royal Icing (page 94)
6–7 pale-coloured cookies or shortbread
1 tsp matcha powder
1 pink marshmallow (optional)
edible black ink pen or black royal icing (optional)
pink royal icing (optional)
pink candy floss

Note: If using fresh cherry blossoms, rinse and use them straightaway. If using pickled cherry blossoms, soak them in water for 10 minutes, then rinse to remove most of the salt.

Can be made vegan!

1 / Preheat the oven to 170°C [340°F/Gas mark 3]. Grease an 18-cm [7-in] diameter round cake tin with butter and line the base with baking paper.

2 / Spoon 80g [3oz] of the Vanilla Cake or Vegan Vanilla Cake batter into a separate bowl, add the cocoa powder and mix until combined evenly. Transfer to a piping [pastry] bag and cut a small tip.

Add the pink sprinkles to the larger amount of white batter and fold in a few times (it doesn't need to be evenly distributed).

3 / Spoon a third of the white and pink batter into the prepared cake tin, then pipe the brown batter in squiggles on the top. Add more white and pink batter on top; gently avoid moving the brown batter too much, and repeat until all the batter has been used up. Ideally, wrap the cake tin with a wet cake strip or towel (page 29) to avoid it doming too much in the centre and bake for 25–30 minutes until springy on top and a skewer inserted into the centre of the cake comes out clean.

4 / Meanwhile, make the chocolate shortbread tree bark. Line a baking sheet (one you can fit in the freezer) with baking paper. Place the butter and sugar in a stand mixer fitted with a balloon whisk attachment (or use a handheld electric whisk/beat with a spatula if your butter is soft enough) and whisk on medium speed until it's a spreadable soft consistency. Add the flour and cocoa powder and mix by hand until just combined. The dough should be slightly sticky, but soft and easy to handle. If necessary, wrap the dough in plastic wrap and chill in the fridge for 10–15 minutes until firm enough to roll out.

5 / Turn the dough out onto a well-floured work surface and roll out until it is 5mm [¼in] thick. Cut out 3 bark-shaped pieces, about 13cm [5in] tall, and place on the lined baking sheet. Then, freeze for 10–15 minutes, while you preheat the oven to 160°C [325°F/Gas mark 3].

6 / Bake the bark shapes for 10–15 minutes. They will be slightly soft but will firm up within minutes of coming out of the oven. Leave to cool for 10 minutes on the baking sheet, then gently transfer to a wire rack to finish cooling.

7 / Add the sakura extract (or alternative) to your chosen buttercream to flavour it.

8 / Using a serrated knife, level the cooled cake and place on a serving tray. Cover the cake with a layer of smooth buttercream. Place a sheet of food-grade acetate (it needs to be 5cm [2in] taller than the buttercream) around the circumference of the cake, pressing it against the buttercream sides. Use a peg or similar to clip the acetate edges together, then use a spatula to fill in any buttercream gaps on the top, so there is no visible buttercream gap between the cake and acetate. If you have an entremet ring, place this tightly around the acetate to help keep it in place and as an extra security for the jelly. If you have used a springform tin to bake the cake, you can also place the outer ring from this around the acetate. Chill the cake in the freezer for 10 minutes.

9 / Meanwhile, assemble the chocolate shortbread tree. Cut 2 of the bark-shaped pieces in half lengthways and, using the Royal Icing, stick them together with the other piece so they stand upright.

10 / When the buttercream is chilled, make the cherry blossom jelly. Add the water, sugar and agar agar powder to a pan and stir to mix in the agar powder. Add a tiny dab of pink food dye to colour. You don't need much, just a slight pink tint. Keep stirring over a high heat until all the sugar has dissolved and the mixture comes to the boil. Leave the mixture to cool down to 45°C [113°F] (if you don't have a thermometer, you should be able to dip your finger in and it won't be too hot that you need to quickly remove your finger),

11 / Pour a thin layer of the cooled jelly on top of the cake. Leave to set in the fridge for about 10 minutes. It will set very quickly as agar agar sets at room temperature. Keep the rest of the agar mixture above 45°C [113°F] to prevent it setting in the pan. Once set on top of the cake, arrange a few cherry blossoms on top of the set jelly and place the shortbread tree in the centre. Add the rest of the jelly in 2 stages, leaving the jelly to set again in between each stage. You can also add more cherry blossoms after the second layer of jelly.

12 / Crush the cookies in a food processor or place in a bag and bash with a rolling pin. Add matcha powder to the bag, seal again and shake to colour the crumbs green. Decorate the base of the cake and up the buttercreamed sides with the crushed green cookie crumbs.

13 / You can also make a marshmallow pig to decorate (though this is optional). Pipe royal icing for the nose area and leave to set, or use pink marzipan or fondant, sticking down with a little royal icing. Use an edible black ink pen or black royal icing to add a face to a pink marshmallow, then use pink royal icing to add the ears and tail.

14 / Just before serving, add the candy floss to the top of the tree. The candy floss will shrink and become sticky as it absorbs moisture from the air, so for the wow factor, serve the cake just after adding the candy floss.

Shrove Tuesday: Semlor Cat Buns

In Sweden, these delicious buns are a treat served on Fat Tuesday (Shrove Tuesday), although many bakeries will stock these right after Christmas and until Lent. They are a delicious flavour combination of cardamom, marzipan and fresh cream, and are extra cute decorated as cats – who also want to celebrate Fat Tuesday!

Can be made vegan!

MAKES: 16–20

DOUGH
120ml [½ cup] milk (or plant-based milk to make vegan)
50g [3½ Tbsp] butter (or vegan butter to make vegan)
120ml [½ cup] water
1 large egg (or 2 Tbsp aquafaba and 1 Tbsp vegetable oil to make vegan)
65g [¼ cup plus 1 Tbsp] caster or granulated sugar
500g [3¾ cups] strong white flour, plus extra for dusting (optional)
1½ tsp ground cardamom (for the best flavour, use fresh cardamon seeds, ground to a fine powder)
1 tsp salt
7-g [¼-oz] sachet fast-action dried [active-dry] yeast

ALMOND PASTE/ MARZIPAN FILLING
(or you can use store-bought marzipan)
125g [¾ cup plus 2 Tbsp] icing [confectioners'] sugar
125g [1¼ cups] ground almonds
1 egg white (or 40g [2⅔ Tbsp] aquafaba to make vegan)
¼ tsp almond extract
¾ tsp amaretto (optional)

CREAM FILLING
500ml [2 cups plus 2 Tbsp] double [heavy] cream (or soy or oat whipping cream to make vegan)
125g [¾ cup plus 2 Tbsp] icing [confectioners'] sugar
1 tsp vanilla bean paste
orange gel food dye

PLUS
sunflower or other neutral-tasting oil, for oiling
1 extra egg, beaten (or 4 parts plant-based milk to 1 part golden syrup [light corn syrup]) for egg wash
orange candy melts/ chocolate buttons or orange fondant
¼ quantity of Royal Icing (page 94)
black gel food dye
orange sprinkles

1 / For the dough, heat the milk in the microwave until tepid, then melt the butter in a separate bowl in the microwave. Add all the wet ingredients to a large bowl or stand mixer and whisk together. Add the sugar and whisk again. Add the flour, cardamom, salt and yeast (on opposites side of bowl to the salt). If using a stand mixer, just attach the dough hook and let the machine knead for about 8 minutes, or until the dough is smooth and elastic. If working by hand, first use a spoon to stir the wet and dry ingredients together until it forms a rough ball of dough. Turn the dough out onto a floured work surface and knead by hand until it is smooth and elastic.

2 / Place the dough into a lightly oiled bowl and cover with lightly oiled plastic wrap. Leave to rise at room temperature for 1–2 hours 30 minutes until doubled in size. The time for this will vary depending on the temperature of the room.

3 / When the dough has risen, line a large baking sheet with baking paper. Divide the dough into individual balls, each one about 45–50g [1½–1¾oz]. Use your hands to shape each one so that it is smooth and taut on top, by stretching the dough and tucking it neatly underneath. Place on to the lined baking sheet and cover with lightly oiled plastic wrap.

Leave to prove at room temperature for 1 hour, or until almost doubled in size and when pressed with a finger the indent slowly comes back up halfway. Preheat the oven to 180°C [350°F/Gas mark 4] halfway through the rising time of the buns.

4 / When risen, brush with the beaten egg (or the milk and golden syrup mixture if making vegan ones) and bake for 15–20 minutes until a deep golden brown on top. Transfer to a wire rack and leave to cool completely.

5 / Meanwhile, make the almond paste. Stir the icing sugar and ground almonds together in a bowl. Add the egg white (or aquafaba), almond extract and amaretto (if using) and stir together until it forms a paste. Set aside for now.

6 / When the buns are cool, whip the double cream (or soy or oat whipping cream), icing sugar and vanilla bean paste together. Add a little orange food dye to colour, then transfer the majority of the cream to a large piping [pastry] bag and cut a large opening. Transfer the rest of the cream to a small piping bag and cut a small opening.

7 / Cut the tops of the buns off and scoop out 2 teaspoons of the insides. Spoon a teaspoon of the almond paste into the bottom of each bun. Use the large piping bag to pipe cream into the bun, then top with the bread lid.

8 / Cut orange candy melts (or chocolate buttons or fondant) into little triangles and press onto the cream for the nose. Make larger triangles in the same way for the ears. Add black food dye to the Royal Icing to achieve the right colour. Transfer to a piping bag and cut a very small tip. Use this to add the cat's eyes and mouth. Poke orange sprinkles into the sides for the whiskers. Use the smaller piping bag of cream to add the cat's paws. Repeat with all the buns. It's fun to make them in various sizes and with different expressions!

Mardi Gras: Cookie Masks & Violet Ganache Macarons

Here are some cookie masks to celebrate the mask wearing and costumes of Mardi Gras parades and festivities, and macarons in the traditional colours of Mardi Gras: purple (representing justice), green (representing faith) and yellow/gold (representing power). Make these a day or so before you want to eat them.

MAKES: 12 MASKS AND AROUND 18 MACARONS

COOKIE MASKS

1 quantity of Ginger and Orange cookie dough (page 94)
1 quantity of Royal icing (page 94)
green, purple and yellow food dyes
a little extra egg white
edible gold paint (optional)
edible gold leaf

VIOLET GANACHE FILLING

160ml [¾ cup minus 1 Tbsp] double [heavy] cream
1¼ Tbsp cornflour [cornstarch]
70g [⅓ cup plus 1 tsp] caster or granulated sugar
100g [¾ cup] white chocolate, finely chopped

100g [7 Tbsp] salted butter, room temperature and cubed
¼ tsp violet essence (though your strength of violet essence may vary, so add to taste)
purple food dye

MACARONS

see page 176
purple, green and yellow food dyes

1 / For the cookie masks, roll out the cookie dough (see page 94). Make a 11 x 4.5-cm [4¼ x 1¾-in] cardboard template for the mask shape, then place this on the dough and cut around the shape. Make 12 masks, then bake and cool according to page 94.

2 / Make the Royal Icing and adjust so it's a thick but pipeable consistency (test a small amount in a piping [pastry] bag). Divide the icing between 3 bowls and colour green, purple and yellow. Transfer 1 heaped tsp or so of each mixture into 3 different piping bags and cut a very small tip (the smaller the tip, the easier it is to control). This will be your icing for outlining and detailed lines. Add a tiny amount extra of egg white to the mixtures remaining in the bowls to make the consistency slightly more fluid, but it should still hold a trail for about 10 seconds. Transfer these to piping

bags and cut a small tip again (although larger than for the outline icing). This will be your 'flood' icing (the icing used to fill the big areas between the lines and cover the cookie). You will have 6 piping bags in total.

3 / For each mask, use the outline icing to mark out lines for the eyes, then pipe a border around the whole mask. Try to squeeze the bag and lift and guide the icing into place, don't try to use it like you would a pen! Use the flood icing to fill in the centre, using a cocktail stick [toothpick] or similar to pop any bubbles and guide the icing into all the edges. Leave to set completely overnight before adding the details on top, because then if you make any mistakes on top, you can just wipe them off and not mess up the first layer. Just create patterns and lines using the outline icing and add a little gold paint on any set icing, if liked.

4 / For the violet ganache filling, mix 30ml [2 Tbsp] of the cream and the cornflour together in a small bowl. Add the remaining cream and the sugar to a small pan and whisk in the cornflour mixture. Stir over a low-medium heat until thickened. Remove from the heat and add the white chocolate, then stir until melted and smooth. Gradually add the butter, a cube at a time, and stir well after each addition, then add the violet flavouring (check for taste) and purple food dye to achieve a lilac colour. When smooth and all incorporated, transfer to a bowl, cover with plastic wrap and chill in the fridge for 1–2 hours until it is firm enough to spread but still holds its shape.

5 / Make the macaron batter following the instructions on pages 176–179. Line 2 baking sheets with baking paper or use a silicone mat. Divide the batter into 3 bowls and colour them purple, green and yellow respectively. Spoon each coloured batter into a different piping bag and knot the tops. Cut the tips, then quickly place all 3 bags into a larger piping bag. Place them all in at the same time, so that they are all at the same height. Snip the end of the large

piping bag (or use a round tip) and pipe in the same way as on page 179. You should see the coloured batter swirl together as you flick the piping bag away. Bang the sheet on a flat surface about 3 times. You should see air bubbles come to the surface. Some of them might pop of their own accord, but you might have to use a cocktail stick to help pop a few. There's no need to add any extra layers after this.

6 / Leave for at least 1–2 hours to form a proper skin on the surface – you should be able to gently touch the macaron and it shouldn't come away on your finger. The time it takes for the macarons to form a skin depends on how humid the air is, so it could take longer. When the macarons are ready to bake, preheat the oven to 150°C [300°F/Gas mark 2] and bake for 15 minutes.

7 / Leave the macarons to cool before peeling them off the baking paper and then sandwich each macaron with the violet ganache filling. Stick some edible gold leaf on top of the macarons with the help of just the tiniest amount of water on the end of a paintbrush. The macarons are best chilled in the fridge for a day or so before serving, as this helps to soften the shell.

Holi: Colour Cake

This cake is a burst of colour for the most colourful of festivals! Not just vibrant on the outside, but when you cut into this cake you have a second colourful surprise – a rainbow of specks from the sprinkles baked into the actual cake and a sunny mango curd oozing out while contrasting with the white buttercream.

Can be made vegan!

SERVES: 25–30 (MAKES: 5 X 18-CM [7-IN] CAKES)

MANGO CURD
(this makes quite a large quantity so you will have some leftover to enjoy!)
8 medium egg yolks
30g [2½ Tbsp] caster or granulated sugar (adjust to taste, depending on sweetness of mango)
10g [2 tsp] cornflour [cornstarch]
500g [3 cups] canned mango pulp
juice of ½ lemon
150g [⅔ cup] salted butter

VEGAN MANGO CURD
150ml [⅔ cup minus 2 tsp] whole coconut milk
pinch of salt, to taste
30g [2½ Tbsp] caster or granulated sugar
40g [½ cup minus 2 tsp] cornflour [cornstarch]
500g [3 cups] mango, peeled and puréed
juice of ½ lemon
50g [¼ cup] coconut oil

PLUS
1 quantity of the batter for the Crème Brûlée Cake (page 15), Vanilla Cake (page 10) or Vegan Vanilla Cake (page 23)
200g [¾ cup plus 4 tsp] rainbow jimmies sprinkles (other sprinkles such as non-pareils may bleed into the cake so jimmies are ideal as they won't bleed and will still look vibrant after baking!), plus extra to decorate
1 quantity of American Buttercream (page 31) or Italian Meringue Buttercream (page 32)
gel food dyes (the more vibrant the better!)

1 – for the mango curd / Put everything except the butter in a heatproof bowl set over a pan of simmering water, making sure the base of the bowl doesn't touch the water. Whisk constantly while heating until the mixture becomes thick. It may take a while to thicken, then it will suddenly get thicker. Once very thick and no longer thickening, remove from the heat and add the butter. Stir until melted and mixed in. Place in a bowl and lay a sheet of plastic wrap directly on the surface of the curd to prevent a skin forming. Refrigerate for a few hours while you make the cake. It will thicken as it cools.

1 – for the vegan mango curd / Make the curd in the same way as above, then add the coconut oil at the end instead of butter. Place in a bowl and lay a sheet of plastic wrap directly on the surface of the curd to prevent a skin forming.

2 / Fold the sprinkles into your chosen cake batter right at the end, then bake and cool following the main cake instructions.

3 / Make sure the cakes are cool before assembling. Stack and crumb-coat the cakes (see pages 27–28) but between each cake layer, pipe an even layer of buttercream, then pipe a dam (page 27) and spoon the mango curd into the centre of each layer. Once the crumb-coated cake is chilled, spread another layer of buttercream all over using a palette knife and smooth the sides and top again. Chill in the fridge until firm again.

4 / Place a few Tbsp of buttercream into 5 different small bowls and add different vibrant gel food dyes to each of these. Use a palette knife to apply the different colours in random abstract strokes

5 / Spread the leftover buttercream in rows onto plastic wrap and roll up into a sausage shape. Cut the end of the plastic wrap, then place into a piping [pastry] bag fitted with a large 1M or 2D piping tip and pipe swirls all around the top of the cake. Scatter with sprinkles, then press sprinkles to the sides of the cake to embellish.

Rio Carnival: Brigadeiros

In Brazil, any celebration is a good excuse to make these addictive, fudge-like chocolate bites. So, of course, brigadeiros is a must at carnival, and this version is fitting for this colourful celebration. There are so many different flavours you can try, as well as endless decorating options, and the actual recipe is so simple (as you can see from the short method!). Just pop all the ingredients into a pan and stir! All you need is a little bit of patience while stirring the ingredients on the stove (you can't walk away otherwise the base will burn!), but you will be rewarded by these fun sprinkle-covered tasty bites.

> Can be made vegan!

MAKES: AROUND 16

30g [2 Tbsp] salted butter (or use vegan butter, ideally over 75% fat content), plus extra for greasing

400g [1¾ cups] sweetened condensed milk (or use coconut-based condensed milk to make vegan)

30g [⅓ cup] unsweetened cocoa powder (replace with vanilla bean paste for a white version, which pairs well with citrus, floral and fruit flavours)

FLAVOUR ADDITIONS & VARIATIONS

- grated zest of 2 oranges, lemons or any citrus fruit for an extra zesty flavour
- ground spices like cinnamon or chilli powder for a spicy kick
- freeze-dried fruit powder or pieces for concentrated fruit flavour without affecting the consistency of the mixture
- nut pastes for a nutty flavour
- rose water, orange blossom water, almond extract or any other concentrated extracts

Tip: For the best flavour, add these right at the end and check for taste.

PLUS

various colourful sprinkles and sparkling sugar sprinkles (small, fine sprinkles work best. The 'sparkling sugar' sprinkles have many names e.g. glitter sugar, shimmer sugar, sanding sugar, but it's basically very fine crystal-like sprinkles which come in lots of different colours.

Tip: Opaque sprinkles work best for chocolate brigadeiros, and shimmery/semi-translucent sparkling sugar sprinkles look best on the white brigadeiros, as the colour stands out. Alternatively, you can roll these in toasted desiccated [shredded] coconut, crunchy chocolate sprinkles (this is more traditional), chopped nuts or cocoa powder – if it sticks to the outside and tastes good, you can use it to coat these!

1 / Grease a large plate with butter.

2 / Place the butter, condensed milk and cocoa powder (or vanilla bean paste) in a small pan and melt over a low heat, stirring constantly with a spatula to avoid burning on the base of the pan. Keep making sure that you are scraping the base and moving the mixture around. You will start to see the it gradually thicken – when you can see the base of the pan for 2–3 seconds when dragging through with the spatula, it is ready. This takes 10–15 minutes.

3 / Transfer the mixture to the prepared plate and chill in the fridge for about 1 hour, or until cold.

4 / Have bowls of sprinkles or sparkling sugar ready. Once chilled, lightly grease your fingertips with butter, then shape the mixture into about 20-g [¾-oz] balls, rolling them between the palms of your hands to make them smooth. Once rolled into a ball, roll in the sprinkles until coated all over. You can pop them into mini cupcake cases (or similar) and store in the fridge if not eaten straightaway!

Pancake Day: Pigs in the Mud

Pancake Day calls for a an extra special pancake stack to wow (imagine waking up to a stack of these in bed?!) – the only problem is that everyone will want to hog this to themselves rather than share.

> Can be made vegan!

SERVES: 4

MACARONS

(This makes a lot more than you need for decorating the pancakes, but you can sandwich them with ganache and serve them separately. See Mardi Gras Macarons on page 169 for a white ganache filling – you can omit the violet flavouring and add flavouring of your choice)

MIXTURE A

105g [1 cup] finely ground and sifted almonds
105g [¾ cup plus 2½ Tbsp] sifted icing [confectioners'] sugar
40g [1½oz] egg white (or aquafaba)

MIXTURE B

45g [1½oz] egg white (or aquafaba)
115g [½ cup plus 1¼ Tbsp] caster or granulated sugar
40ml [2⅔ Tbsp] water

PANCAKES

435g [3⅓ cups] plain [all-purpose] flour
75g [6 Tbsp] caster or granulated sugar
6 tsp baking powder
⅓ tsp salt
1 tsp vanilla bean paste
3 medium eggs
450ml [2 cups minus 2 Tbsp] whole milk

VEGAN PANCAKES

435g [3⅓ cups] plain [all-purpose] flour
75g [6 Tbsp] caster or granulated sugar

6 tsp baking powder
⅓ tsp salt
1 tsp vanilla bean paste
555ml [2⅓ cups] soy or almond milk
3 tsp vegetable oil

PLUS

edible black pen
oil or butter, for frying pancakes
your choice of filling: butter, maple syrup, etc!
200g [1 cup plus 2 Tbsp] dark [bittersweet] chocolate, melted
sprinkles

1 / First, make the pig macarons. Line 2 baking sheets with baking paper or a silicone mat. It helps to use a silicone mat that has circle templates already printed on it, although this isn't essential. You can also slide a hand-drawn template underneath your baking paper. Also, have all your piping [pastry] bags and any pink food dye you will be using ready to hand.

2 / For Mixture A, stir the sifted ground almonds and icing sugar together in a large bowl. Add the egg white (or aquafaba) and mix together until it forms a paste.

3 / For Mixture B, add the egg white (or aquafaba) to a stand mixer fitted with the balloon whisk attachment (or use a handheld electric whisk).

4 / Add the caster sugar and water to a pan and stir occasionally over a medium-high heat until the sugar has dissolved and the mixture starts to bubble. Start whisking the egg white (or aquafaba) to soft peaks. You want to time the sugar syrup reaching 115°C [239°F] with the egg white (or aquafaba) reaching soft peaks. You can always take the sugar syrup off the stove and/or slow the mixer (but don't turn it off) to time the two together.

Tip: The aquafaba will take longer to whisk to soft peaks than the egg whites, so bear this in mind when timing this with the sugar syrup reaching 115°C [239°F].

5 / When the egg white (or aquafaba) has reached soft peaks and the sugar syrup is at 115°C [239°F], increase the speed of the mixer (or whisk) to high while pouring the sugar syrup in a thin stream down the side of the bowl (do not pour directly onto the whisk).

6 / Once all the sugar has been poured in, continue whisking on high speed until the side of the bowl feels cool to the touch, 3–5 minutes or so. At this point, turn off the mixer and use a spatula to fold the meringue into Mixture A. Add pink food dye to colour, then transfer to a piping bag fitted with a large round piping tip (or cut a large tip). Leave some batter behind, transfering this to a smaller piping bag.

7 / Pipe the macarons onto the prepared baking sheets in simple round shapes. If the macaron batter is the correct consistency, the macarons should spread slightly after piping but still hold their shape, and the tip of the macarons should disappear within a minute or so.

8 / After piping, pick up the baking sheets and bang it on a flat surface about 3 times. You should see air bubbles come to the surface. Some of them might pop of their own accord, but you might have to use a cocktail stick [toothpick] to help pop a few.

9 / Leave the macarons for about 15 minutes until they form a slight skin, then use the smaller piping bag to add ears and nose. Leave for at least 1–2 hours to form a proper skin on the surface – you should be able to gently touch the macaron and it shouldn't come away on your finger. The time it takes for the macarons to form a skin depends on how humid the air is, so it could take longer.

10 / When the macarons are ready, preheat the oven to 150°C [300°F/Gas mark 2] (or 120°C [250°F/Gas mark ½] for vegan macarons). Bake egg white-based macarons for about 15 minutes or the vegan macarons for 30 minutes. Leave the macarons to cool before peeling them off the baking paper. They are best chilled in the fridge for a day or so before serving, as this helps to soften the shell – this is especially the case for the vegan macarons as they tend to be crunchier due to their longer baking time. Add details using an edible black pen.

11 – for the pancakes / Whisk the flour, sugar, baking powder, salt, vanilla and eggs together in a bowl with a balloon whisk (or use a handheld electric whisk) until smooth. Add the milk and whisk again until smooth.

11 – for the vegan pancakes / Whisk all the ingredients together in a bowl.

12 / Add 1 tsp of oil or a knob of butter to a pan and heat over a medium heat until hot. Add a ladleful of the batter to the pan and spread it out until it is about 12cm [4½in] in diameter. Cook until the edges are looking dry and the bubbles on the surface are beginning to pop. Flip and cook on the other side until golden. Transfer to a plate and repeat until you have used up three-quarters of the batter.

Tip: When cooking the pancakes, keep a close eye on the first pancake to cook it to a golden brown colour on each side. Once the edges of the pancake look dry, you can peek underneath to check the colour before flipping. The second side of the pancake will need cooking for about half as long. After you've made the first and second pancakes, you should have a good feel for the cooking time and temperature for the next ones!

13 / For the pig-shaped pancakes, transfer about a sixth of the remaining batter to a piping bag (or squeezy bottle), then transfer the rest of the batter to a second piping bag (or squeezy bottle). Keep the heat low while you pipe the outlines and details of the pig that you want to show through as darker lines later into the pan using the smaller amount of batter. Leave to cool until the batter looks dry on top (you can carefully peek a little bit underneath to check the colour – you want it to be brown, although bear in mind it will darken while the next layer of pancake batter is cooking), then pipe on the second layer of batter to completely cover the lines. Cook as normal, and hopefully when you flip you will reveal the pig design! This quantity makes about 5 pig pancakes.

14 / Arrange the pancakes in a tall stacked tower. You can add butter and drizzle maple syrup between each layer, then drizzle with the melted chocolate and decorate with the pig-shaped pancakes, macarons and sprinkles.

Oktoberfest: Smiley Pretzels

You can't have Oktoberfest without pretzels, and you can't celebrate without smiling. These expressive pretzels will certainly make you smile when you see them, and smile again when you bite into them.

MAKES: 12

DOUGH
600g [4¼ cups] strong white flour
220ml [1 cup minus 4 tsp] water
100ml [7 Tbsp] whole milk (or plant-based milk)
50g [3½ Tbsp] butter, softened (or vegan butter)
1½ Tbsp caster or granulated sugar
7-g [¼-oz] sachet fast-action dried [active-dry] yeast
1 Tbsp salt

SOLUTION
1 litre [4 cups plus 3 Tbsp] boiling water
3 Tbsp bicarbonate of soda [baking soda]

PLUS
sunflower or other neutral-tasting oil, for oiling
coarse sea salt, for sprinkling
a little Royal Icing (page 94) or 30g [3½ Tbsp] icing [confectioners'] sugar
edible eyes

Can be made vegan!

1 / Add the dough ingredients to a stand mixer (don't add the salt and yeast on top of each other) and knead on speed 2 with the dough hook attachment. Knead until smooth and elastic and it passes the windowpane test. You can also knead this by hand; add the ingredients, then mix with a large wooden spoon until roughly combined. Turn out onto a work surface and knead until smooth and elastic.

Note: For the windowpane test, tear off a small piece of dough, flatten it, then stretch it thinly between your fingertips. If you can stretch it into a thin membrane, hold it up to a window and see light through it, then your dough is properly kneaded and the gluten has developed enough. If it tears, knead it for longer!

2 / Place the dough in a lightly oiled bowl and cover with lightly oiled plastic wrap. Leave to rise for 1–2 hours at room temperature (depending on the ambient temperature) until it has doubled in size.

3 / Knock back the dough and divide into 12 pieces. Roll each piece into a sausage about 50cm [20in] long, with the ends tapered and the middle wider. Hold both tapered ends upwards and twist them over each other twice, then bring them back down and attach the ends to the sides of the pretzel. Press to make sure they are stuck down. Rise, uncovered, for 30 minutes, or until when lightly pressed the dough gradually comes back most of the way but not totally.

4 / Just before the pretzels have finished rising, preheat the oven to 200°C [400°F/Gas mark 6]. Prepare the solution by pouring the boiling water into a large pan and adding the bicarbonate of soda. Carefully place a pretzel on a large slotted spoon and immerse in the water for about 5 seconds. Remove to a baking sheet. Repeat with all the pretzels. Sprinkle over coarse sea salt and bake for about 20 minutes, or until dark and glossy.

5 / Leave to cool, then either use Royal Icing or mix the icing sugar with a little water, a drop at a time, until it's pipeable and use to stick on the edible eyes.

Note: You may find that the pretzels you shaped first are risen while the ones shaped later aren't. If you know you will be working slowly, place the finished pretzels in the fridge to rise (the fridge will slow the rise but not stop it) while you work on the next ones.

"Dough something special for yourself every day."

Lantern Festival: Meringues

The Lantern Festival is celebrated on the 15th day of the first month of the lunar calendar in many Asian countries. These hanging meringues are simple to make, but create a great interactive showstopper and talking point when a lot are hung together – maybe over a dining table with a feast below.

> Can be made vegan!

MAKES: 2 LARGE BAKING SHEETS OF MERINGUE LANTERNS

MERINGUE
210g [1 cup plus 2 tsp] caster or granulated sugar
120g [4oz] egg white (or aquafaba)
pinch of cream of tartar (optional)
gel food dyes

PLUS
30g [3½ Tbsp] icing [confectioners'] sugar
see-through fishing wire and ribbon

> The method for both regular and vegan meringues is essentially the same, the only difference being that the vegan ones takes a little longer to whip to soft peaks initially, and are best baked until completely dry in the centre. The purpose of baking meringues is to dry them out rather than cook them, so don't be tempted to turn the oven up!

1 / Preheat the oven to 200°C [400°F/Gas mark 6]. Line a baking sheet with baking paper and spread out the sugar. Place in the oven for 7–8 minutes until warm but not caramelized, discarding any bits that are caramelized and replacing with an equal weight of sugar. Remove the tray of sugar from the oven, and leave the oven door open to allow it to cool down to 100°C [212°F/Gas mark ¼], ready for the meringues to bake.

2 / Add the egg white (or aquafaba) to a stand mixer fitted with a balloon whisk attachment (you can use a handheld electric whisk but you will be whisking for a long time so a stand mixer is ideal). Mix on high speed until you have soft peaks, then gradually add the sugar, 1 Tbsp at a time, whisking for about 30–60 seconds after each addition. It is important to add the sugar very slowly so that it all dissolves.

3 / When all the sugar has been incorporated (the meringue should feel smooth and not gritty between your fingers), add the cream of tartar (if using), then divide the mixture between bowls and colour as

desired. Use a spatula to transfer the meringue to piping [pastry] bags fitted with a sultane tip.

4 / Pipe shapes onto baking paper or a silicone mat (you need to pull upwards slowly to get the best shape, but you will quickly get used to it!) and bake for 1 hour 30 minutes. Switch the oven off and leave the oven door closed for a few hours until the meringues are completely crisp and dry. You can bake 2 sheets at a time.

5 / To assemble, mix the icing sugar with a few drops of water, a drop at a time, in a bowl to make a thick paste. Place in a piping bag and cut a small tip. Sandwich 2 meringues together using the icing, then tie up with the fishing wire like a criss-crossed parcel, so that the meringue is balanced on both sides. Attach the ribbon to the top and hang up!

Note: Attaching the ribbon to the meringues can be fiddly work, although it's very rewarding to have all of these strung up to create an amazing hanging edible decoration. It helps if you are patient and good at doing knots!

Songkran: Water Island Cake

Songkran is Thailand's most famous festival and is at the beginning of the Thai New Year in April. Throwing water and water fights have become a big part of the festivities, so this water beach cake is here to celebrate that! Feel free to try to base this landscape on your favourite beach.

Can be made vegan!

SERVES: 12

GANACHE
450g [16oz] dark [bittersweet chocolate] chocolate (at least 70% cocoa solids), finely chopped
180ml [¾ cup] double [heavy] cream (or coconut milk to make vegan)

CHOCOLATE CAKE
½ quantity of the Chocolate Cake (page 14) or Vegan Chocolate Cake (page 25), baked in 2 x 18-cm [7-in] cake tins and cooled

JELLY
800ml [3⅓ cups] water
140g [¾ cup minus 2 tsp] caster or granulated sugar
1¾ tsp agar agar powder
turquoise gel food dye
large pieces of peel of 1 orange and 1 lemon

PLUS
80g [3oz] white chocolate, for filling seashell moulds and brushing onto ganache sea bed
any pale-coloured cookies, to crush
matcha powder
white liquid food dye
edible flowers (optional)

1 / Prepare the decorations for later. Melt the white chocolate in 15-second bursts in the microwave, then use to fill miniature silicone seashell moulds. Chill in the freezer and turn out and use just before needed. These will need to stay very cold as the chocolate isn't being tempered. Set the rest of the melted chocolate aside for later.

2 / Crush the cookies in a food processor or place in a bag and bash with a rolling pin. Place in a few different bowls. Leave 1 bowl plain, then colour another green using matcha powder (you can create 2 different shades of green if you like).

Note: These are all just suggestions to start with, but you can experiment with different-coloured seashells, or place other creations into the sea – maybe sunken treasure at the bottom, a boat on the surface of the water, or something unexpected. You can also make green sponge cake in addition to the crushed cookies for a different textural effect.

3 / Next, for the ganache, place the chocolate in a large heatproof bowl. Heat the cream (or coconut milk) in a pan on the stove, until JUST starting to bubble around the edges, then pour it onto the chocolate. Leave for 2 minutes, then stir until all the chocolate has melted. If there are still pieces of unmelted chocolate, transfer back to a pan and return to the stove. Stir over a low heat until all the chocolate has melted (or place in microwave for very short 5–10-second bursts). When smooth, leave to cool until it is a nice spreadable consistency.

4 / Take your cooled cakes. Use a serrated knife to cut the top off one cake, so it is flat. Place on a serving tray and spread a layer of ganache on top. Place the second cake layer on top, then carve the cake so that it roughly resembles the island you want to create. You can use trimmed cake pieces to add more height in some areas, using the ganache to stick them together. Ensure there's a variety of tall areas for mountains and lower areas to be covered

by the sea. You can carve the cake as low as you like, although leave a bit of cake at the bottom so that it remains round. Cover the exposed cake with ganache (you can be messy here, it doesn't need to be very smooth) and chill in the fridge until firm.

5 / When the cake is chilled, use a paintbrush to dab on the reserved melted white chocolate (it may need a few seconds in the microwave to melt again) all over the ganache that will be beneath the 'sea'. Create a mottled effect rather than painting the chocolate as one block colour. Use a paintbrush with some white liquid food dye to add dimension to the mountain areas of the island. You can add more later, so it doesn't need to be perfect yet. Chill in the fridge until set.

6 / Once set, arrange some of your decorations on the seabed, such as the edible flowers and chocolate seashells. Decorations nearer the outer circumference of the cake will be more visible. For the decorations that you want in the middle of the sea rather than attached to an edge, these will be added later as the jelly layers build up.

7 / Spread a little extra ganache (this may need a few seconds in the microwave to make it spreadable again) around the exposed areas around the circumference of the base of the cake, then place a sheet of clear food-grade acetate around the whole cake, pressing to stick it to the ganache all the way around (otherwise it may leak!). Use a clip or tape to hold the overlapping acetate ends together. If you used a cake tin with a removable base, then place the outer circle around the acetate to help hold it in place, or you can use an adjustable entremet ring. Place the cake back in the fridge while you make the jelly.

8 / For the jelly, add the water, sugar and agar agar powder to a pan and stir to disperse the powder. Add a very small amount of turquoise food dye to colour (use the end of a cocktail stick [toothpick] to avoid adding too much). Add the citrus peel and stir occasionally over a high heat until the sugar and agar agar have dissolved, then bring to the boil. As soon as it's boiling, remove from the heat and take out the citrus peel.

9 / The jelly will start to set between 40–45°C [104–113°F], so you want to pour it onto the cake just before this. It also needs to be poured in layers, each layer setting before adding the next. This forms a nice seal so the jelly doesn't just leak out. Once the first layer of jelly is set, you know you're safe to keep going! The layering of the jelly also allows you to place decorative items in the jelly so that they aren't all just at the bottom or at the sides. The easiest way to do this is to pour a small amount of liquid into a measuring jug or cup, and wait for this to cool to between 45–48°C [113–118°F], then pour in. It should set very quickly after pouring in. The heat of the pan and volume of liquid in there should keep the main mixture from cooling too fast, although if it does you can just put it back on the lowest heat setting. Keep repeating, pouring a small amount into a bowl to cool, and pouring in layers. Add decorations wherever you would like them.

10 / Once you've added your jelly to the height you would like it and it has set firm, peel off the acetate and reveal your handiwork! Now just decorate to your heart's content! Brush on white food dye to look like spray on the edges of water, then use the uncoloured cookie crumbs for a beach, green crumbs to represent forest and add in whatever you would like to create your beach scene.

INDEX

Acknowledgements

I've always thought that people who bake are some of the nicest people ever, because we want to put time in creating something that will bring a moment of happiness to others. So thank YOU all, you kind bakers out there, for spreading happiness around! Plus I LOVE seeing all your amazing creations born from my recipes!

To my three main cheerleaders and taste testers – my partner Nabil and our two rescue cats Inki and Mochi – thank you all for your excellent feedback. Inki and Mochi – your feedback mainly consisted of 'meow' to cream and butter, and no interest in anything else, so I had to ignore it from time to time. But you're furry and keep me company so I forgive you.

Also thank you to my weird and wonderful family (Kenneth have you tried any of my recipes yet?) and friends (let's have a cake party soon please!)

Special mentions to Céline Hughes, Alicia House, Ellis Parrinder, Sarah Hardy and Charlotte Love. You all have been a joy to work with (though it didn't feel like work!) and the best team members I could ask for. I am also so grateful to Linda van den Berg, Danni Hooker, Mary Kate McDevitt and Vivienne Clore.

Thanks to everyone else who has been amazing – you know who you are and I need to bake a giant cake for you all soon!

PUBLISHING DIRECTOR: Sarah Lavelle
SENIOR COMMISSIONING EDITOR: Céline Hughes
EDITORIAL ASSISTANT: Sofie Shearman
DESIGNER: Alicia House
PHOTOGRAPHER: Ellis Parrinder
ASSISTANT FOOD STYLIST: Sarah Hardy
PROP STYLIST: Charlotte Love
HAIR & MAKE-UP: Danni Hooker
HEAD OF PRODUCTION: Stephen Lang
PRODUCTION CONTROLLER: Katie Jarvis

Published in 2021 by Quadrille,
an imprint of Hardie Grant Publishing

QUADRILLE
52–54 Southwark Street
London SE1 1UN
quadrille.com

Cataloguing in Publication Data: a catalogue record for this book is available from the British Library.

Text © Kim-Joy 2021
Photography © Ellis Parrinder 2021
Design and layouts © Quadrille 2021

ISBN 978 1 78713 789 9

Printed in China